What People Are Saying About
Finding Your Voice

"*Finding Your Voice* will prove to be an excellent resource. . . .
Written in a personal, conversational style. . . . A book with a profound
understanding of the need for leadership in a democracy."
—Robert L. Payton, professor of philanthropic studies, Indiana University

"All of us are leaders—in our families, communities, churches and
synagogues, and workplaces. Jam-packed with practical advice
and wisdom, this is the leadership book for you."
**—Perry M. Smith, president, Visionary Leadership, Ltd.,
military analyst for CNN, and author of *Taking Charge***

"As citizens, every one of us has the opportunity to make a difference—
to identify a problem or opportunity in our community and provide
leadership in doing something about it. In *Finding Your Voice*,
Dr. Matusak blends leadership concepts with practical experience
to help us do so, and she uses a language we all understand!
Must reading for all who care enough to lead."
—Russell G. Mawby, chairman emeritus, W.K. Kellogg Foundation

"Demystifies leadership and places it within the realm of the possible."
**—Gill Robinson Hickman, professor of leadership studies,
University of Richmond**

"The right book for a nation indebted to citizen leaders for its
glorious past and in great need of more of them to deal with
the staggering challenges of its future."
**—Brian O'Connell, professor of public service,
Filene Center for Citizenship and Public Affairs, Tufts University**

"A top-to-bottom study of leadership written by one of the country's
foremost leadership scholars. Both readable and profound—
it should be in every briefcase and knapsack in America."
**—Georgia Sorenson, Center for Political Leadership
and Participation, University of Maryland**

"*Finding Your Voice* bridges the gap between the theory and practice
of leadership with inspiring examples and practical tools."
—Nancy Axelrod, president, National Center for Nonprofit Boards

"A wonderful guide to discovering the leadership potential within each
of us. If you have a passion to make a difference but require a bit of
encouragement to get started, this is a MUST book for you!"
—Dr. Roger H. Sublett, director, Kellogg National Leadership Program

Publication Sponsored by the W.K. Kellogg Foundation

The W.K. Kellogg Foundation was founded in 1930 with a clear mission: "To help people help themselves through the practical application of knowledge and resources to improve their quality of life and that of future generations." The private foundation that began funding programs to meet the health and educational needs of Michigan children has grown to a position of national and international prominence for its assistance to communities in the United States, Latin America, the Caribbean, and southern Africa. Today, the W.K. Kellogg Foundation is one of the largest philanthropic organizations in the world.

As a private grantmaking institution, the W.K. Kellogg Foundation provides seed money to nonprofit organizations and institutions that have identified problems and designed constructive action programs aimed at solutions. Most grants are awarded in the areas of higher education; youth development; leadership, philanthropy, and volunteerism; comprehensive health care systems; and rural development.

Finding Your Voice

Finding Your Voice

Learning to Lead . . . Anywhere You Want to Make a Difference

Larraine R. Matusak

Foreword by Andrew J. Young

A publication of the W.K. Kellogg Foundation

Jossey-Bass Publishers • San Francisco

Substantial discounts on bulk quantities of Jossey-Bass books are available to corporations, professional associations, and other organizations. For details and discount information, contact the special sales department at Jossey-Bass Inc., Publishers (415) 433–1740; Fax (800) 605–2665.

For sales outside the United States, please contact your local Simon & Schuster International Office.

Manufactured in the United States of America on Lyons Falls Pathfinder Tradebook. This paper is acid-free and 100 percent totally chlorine-free.

A Publication of the W.K. Kellogg Foundation

Credits are on pages 193-194.

Library of Congress Cataloging-in-Publication Data

Matusak, Larraine R.
    Finding your voice : learning to lead— anywhere you want to make a difference / Larraine R. Matusak ; foreword by Andrew J. Young.
       p. cm.
    Includes bibliographical references (p.) and index.
    ISBN 0-7879-0305-1 (paper)
    1. Leadership—Handbooks, manuals, etc. 2. Social action—Handbooks, manuals, etc. I. Title.
HM141.M29   1997
303.3'4—dc20   96-25322

PB Printing 10 9 8 7 6 5 4 3 2 1   FIRST EDITION

Contents

To Connie,

whose sense of humor and support
gave me the energy to complete this book,

and to regular citizens all over the country,

who have inspired me with their dedication
and enthusiasm as they make our communities
better places to live and work!

Foreword

Finding Your Voice is just what America needs today. We are a nation faced with a myriad of issues, including violence, crime, public policy conflicts, and behavior that is generally abusive. We are debating whether to feed children and provide medical coverage to all citizens while our country has the best medical facilities in the world and grows enough food to feed a large portion of the world. Yet many Americans are homeless and malnourished and our elderly must choose between paying bills and purchasing medicine.

These issues touch all of us. Generally, we don't know how to get hold of them, even in our own lives. Consequently, we let our lives and our nation drift because we don't know how to take action. We desire change but we think, "I can't make a difference." So we either complain, or worse, remain silent.

Larraine Matusak, in this extraordinary and courageous volume, offers us the chance to grow, to mature as citizens, parents, and friends, by finding and using our voice. To me, finding one's voice is merely the end result of a personal journey in which an individual learns to take risks, to act for self and community, and to be an actor in the daily drama of life well lived. This is essentially the bedrock of grassroots democracy.

This process of producing grassroots leadership is essential to our democracy, yet difficult to capture. I began my journey with Dr. Martin Luther King as the director of the Citizenship School Project, where we identified uneducated people with Ph.D.-caliber minds and offered them training. Many of these people and their children went on to become leaders and elected officials for their newly enfranchised communities. In *Finding Your Voice,* Matusak offers guidance to those who want to be involved in improving their communities and are unsure where to begin. This step-by-step

process of learning how to lead is an invaluable tool to help people answer the question, "What can I do?"

Atlanta, Georgia   ANDREW J. YOUNG
August 1996   Ambassador,
                              Co-chair Atlanta Olympic Committee

Preface

There are already hundreds of leadership books on the market—but this one is not redundant. I spent two years researching and reviewing the bulk of the leadership literature, and that is what convinced me to write this book. Most of the available books are very theoretical and are addressed to a limited audience. They use the language of business or politics and are written primarily to be used in schools of business or political science at the colleges and universities around the country. The examples and language they use to clarify the theory are also those of successful or failing businesses or of political leaders, or people who have led businesses. This implies that the present and future leaders of our country will come only from the world of business or government.

I beg to differ! What about the leaders of the nonprofit world, the homemakers, nurses, artists, schoolteachers, students, volunteers, small business people—*regular people,* who are making impressive strides toward improving our communities? These potential or presently active citizen leaders find very few, if any, leadership books or materials to help them improve their leadership in terms to which they can relate. They need knowledge, encouragement, help, and insight into what will make them more effective citizen leaders.

Audience

I have written this book for all of us, *regular people,* who may or may not be a part of the business community or government, who may not have positions or titles that bring power, but who are eager to learn more or need to be encouraged to learn more about effective leadership and followership.

A secondary audience may be those people who have achieved titles and powerful positions. Through the contents of this book, they may be made aware of the hidden treasures to be found in the many talented and gifted persons who surround them. If they don't already do so, they may even be encouraged to use the inclusive leadership style reflected in the work of the people whose stories are told in the following chapters.

So, if you don't have a title or a position of power, but you want to make a difference, *this book is for you*. It will challenge you to find your voice, discover your passion, and take the risk of accepting leadership opportunities that may come your way. If you do hold a position or title of authority, *this book is for you, too*. It may help you discover the means to become a more effective leader and follower and it may also make you more aware of the power of inclusiveness.

From beginning to end, this book deals with fundamentals. I have not attempted to tease out some new or challenging theory of leadership. My purpose and passion is to bring the knowledge and practice of leadership that is already available to academics and business people to students, young people searching for something meaningful to do, and to the world of all the rest of us. I have tried to make the essential aspects of effective leadership, as I see them, come alive through the people you will meet in these pages. They are real people who have taken it upon themselves to make a difference. I hope that as you read this book you will discover the self you want to be—or the self you already are—but most certainly I hope you will *find your voice* and be the self you were meant to be.

Overview of the Contents

This book has three sections. Part One is dedicated to helping you understand that everyone has the potential to make a difference. The four chapters are designed to help you *find your voice*. You will find many examples of successful citizen leaders. You will meet a homemaker, a priest from Detroit, a senior citizen from California, and a teenager from New England; all are people without titles or lofty positions. You may discover that they are people just like you who have taken the risk of addressing some serious issues! I hope that these examples will inspire you to live your life with the greatest possible creativity, purpose, and potency. I also hope that these chapters will free you from preconceived notions of fear or inferiority. Take time to reflect. Challenge the information. Discover who you really are! Learn the value of effective leadership and supportive followership, and begin to focus on situations where you can become a leader or a more supportive follower.

In Part Two, I have tried to describe the essential elements of leadership and followership. Leadership is a body of knowledge that can be taught and learned by anyone. *Leadership is making a difference.* Leadership is a process of visioning, initiating, guiding, and encouraging a group to accomplish positive change. We can all learn to use these tools. The eight chapters in this section will introduce you to a practical set of tools and examples to help you achieve your goal of effective leadership. You will meet the many impressive people discovered and interviewed in the course of writing this book. Young people, senior people, men and women, energetic people from all parts of the United States who have taken the initiative to make a difference and improve their communities or workplaces. Some have official titles, but the majority do not. They were eager to share their successes, and in some cases failures, with us. From a fireman in Iowa, a senior citizen in Pennsylvania, or a teenager in Michigan to the woman CEO of a technology business—all have lessons for us about effective leadership and followership. Learn from them. Write in the margins, complete the exercises, challenge the ideas, think and grow so that you will be prepared to act.

One of the most essential qualities of leadership is the ability to act, to make it happen, to translate your passion into reality. Introspection and discovering your voice are extremely valuable. Learning about the theory and practical applications of effective leadership are excellent tools. But unless we practice using this knowledge, these tools, there will be no significant outcomes. Part Two concludes by encouraging you to use your insight into yourself and the tools of effective leadership found in Chapters Five through Twelve, to develop a plan of action around an issue that means the most to you. Use it as your road map; it is meant to lead you to clear results. Use it as your growth plan, your record of developing a means to create positive social change for your family, community, or place of employment. Whether you are already in a leadership position or are embarking on your first adventure into the realm of leadership, this section can be a positive experience for you.

At the end of the book, the Resources section directs you to further leadership education programs, books, and audiovisual materials, which may be very helpful on your journey to growth and development.

In a democracy, every citizen has both the option and the responsibility to be a part of the process of improving society. Perhaps, with your help, we can reshape the thinking about leadership and followership so that more and more of us can find and use our voices to create a better future for those who follow us as we approach a new century.

Battle Creek, Michigan   LARRAINE R. MATUSAK
August 1996

Acknowledgments

I have discovered that writing is a very lonely activity. If you are a person who enjoys people, as I do, the daily isolation from a circle of friends and hectic daily activity can lead to many emotional highs and lows. During the period of writing this book, my friends have seen me at my wit's end with frustration or absolutely elated because of a wonderful interview. First among these special people to whom I owe a depth of gratitude and love is Connie Julius, my friend, who was ever patient, understanding, and supportive. I have dedicated this book to her because she has lived with it, through me, for many years as it grew from the tiny seed of an idea to the reality of the writing stages.

James MacGregor Burns and Judith Addington were the first two people to review my outline and encourage me to begin putting my thoughts on paper. Without their positive support, I would probably still be merely talking about the prospect of writing a book. I am deeply grateful to them both.

Special thanks go to my colleagues at the W.K. Kellogg Foundation, Russell G. Mawby, chairman emeritus, and Norman A. Brown, president emeritus, for being excited about the project and giving me the time and support to tackle this challenge. To Gail McClure, Mike Thompson, and Tim Brostrom I owe a depth of gratitude for their understanding and expertise in helping me set up a home office and a mobile office so that the work could be accomplished in environments conducive to reflection and thoughtfulness. They were always as close as my telephone whenever I ran into technological difficulties. I have become quite proficient under their tutelage.

A very special thank-you is extended to all the Kellogg National Fellows and Advisors who sent me the names of hundreds of people all over the United States and abroad who are making a difference without getting their names in the headlines or on television.

Their stories bring the truths of this book to life. I learned years ago that the practice of effective leadership and strong, supportive followership can never be perfected. It must be practiced, experienced, and then practiced again. It takes a lifetime of practice and learning. Very special thanks also go not only to the people whose names and stories appear in the text but also to those whose stories we heard but simply could not include this time. With people like these all over the country, I look forward to the future.

Alice Warner, a W.K. Kellogg program associate, conducted interviews, checked the facts, and secured releases. Her eagle eye kept me honest as I began to construct the stories gathered from lengthy transcriptions and summaries. Her patience, sensitivity, and enthusiasm in tracing leads on people whose stories were valuable to me made what could have been a tedious task a great deal of fun.

Throughout this period of writing, thinking, discussing, and researching, there are two people who have been remarkable colleagues, assistants, cheerleaders, and friends. These two are Michelle Reece, program associate, and Pamela Bruinekool, executive secretary. Michelle had the task of writing diplomatic notes about how I could improve what I had written. She also assumed the responsibility for checking and putting all my references into the proper format. In the midst of all the chaos, she had a beautiful new baby boy. Fortunately for me, Michelle, her husband, Mike, and little Jacob were all committed to the project so that we never missed a beat.

Without Pam, little could have been accomplished in the allotted time. She struggled with incompatible disks; carried tons of material daily from my home office to the foundation offices and back; communicated via electronic mail, fax, UPS, and telephone when I was out of town; and kept my office running smoothly at the foundation. She and Alice carried double duty while Michelle was introduced to motherhood. Her expert eye for detail kept us accurate, and her willingness to tackle every challenge with a positive attitude kept our spirits high. Michelle and Pam are the two people most responsible for getting this book to the publisher on time. I must not omit Pam's husband, Ted, and their three children. Their willingness to have mom work odd hours and make regular stops at my home have not been overlooked. I thank them all from the bottom of my heart.

There are many others—colleagues at the W.K. Kellogg Foundation, KNFP Fellows, friends from universities where I have taught and administered, and neighbors and family members who gave me advice, read chapters, brainstormed ideas, and generally supported the idea of the book. To list them all would be futile because I am apt to forget someone. However, you all know who you are; so, thank you for your support and assistance in making this book a reality. In truth, it belongs to all of you.

When I was first directed to Alan Shrader, senior editor at Jossey-Bass, I didn't know what to expect. His support, frankness, and sense of humor have energized me throughout this process. I also want to say thank you to the many other Jossey-Bass employees who answered our questions and helped us achieve our final goal.

—L.R.M.

The Author

Larraine R. Matusak was born and raised in Chicago. Her first impressions of citizen leadership and the power of understanding how to promote change were experienced in an area called "the back of the yards." She received her B.A. degree (1964) in biology and chemistry from the College of St. Benedict, and her M.A. degree (1968) in entomology from the University of Minnesota, Minneapolis. She received her Ph.D. degree (1974) in higher education administration from The Fielding Institute of Graduate Studies, Santa Barbara, California.

Matusak has been a scholar and practitioner of leadership for many years. She has served in a wide variety of leadership roles. She is a program officer and leadership scholar at the W.K. Kellogg Foundation, where she designed and directed the Kellogg National Fellowship Program, a leadership development program for people in the early years of their career. She also led in the creation of the leadership grantmaking area at the W.K. Kellogg Foundation and then served as the first coordinator for the department. She has served as a consultant to many communities, organizations, academic institutions, and foundations desiring to set up or strengthen leadership development programs. Her creativity and innovative approach to problem solving and leadership have been recognized by educators, business leaders, nonprofit groups, and community organizations.

Matusak served as president of Thomas A. Edison State College in New Jersey and was dean and founder of the College of Alternative Programs at the University of Evansville, Indiana. She was on the original design team and directed the Alternative Baccalaureate Program at the University of Minnesota and was a professor of natural sciences at that institution. She has received numerous honors including the Outstanding American Educator award from the Medical College of Augusta, Georgia, as well as four honorary doctorates.

Matusak has also served on many national and local boards and committees. She is immediate past chairperson of the board of S.A.F.E. Place, a domestic violence shelter for women, and serves on the boards of the Battle Creek Symphony and the Battle Creek Boychoir and Girls' Chorus. She is a board member of the Institute for Leadership Development of the University of Southern California and serves on the board of the Institute for Dialogue of the Massachusetts Institute of Technology.

Finding Your Voice

| Why Not You?

Part One is devoted to helping you understand that everyone has the potential to make a difference. The chapters are designed to help you *find your voice.* I want to try to convince you that every day of your life is filled with opportunities to be creative, to act with purpose and potency. You don't need an elevated position or a title of great importance to assume a leadership role. You do need to discover your own passion and to fit leadership opportunities to your specific talents.

The four chapters in this section are filled with examples of successful citizen leaders who have neither titles nor lofty positions. You may discover that they are people just like you! They are not rich and famous, but they have broken free of their self-constricting perceptions and have been willing to initiate, guide, and encourage others to work with them to accomplish positive change. Chapter One will challenge you to look beyond title, experience, and preconceived notions when talking or thinking about leadership. By meeting regular citizens like Betty, Sarah, Ruth, and others, you will be encouraged to recognize your worth and decide where you can make a contribution. Chapter Two, through stories and an exercise, leads you to discover your passion. Only by discovering what we know, what we care deeply about, and what we still have to learn can we hope to make a positive contribution to society. In Chapter Three, the sensitive subject of followership is addressed. Followership is not demeaning! Leadership and followership are two sides of a single sheet of paper. One cannot exist without the other. Although this may be a difficult idea to accept, it is necessary to discuss if we are to arrive at a clear understanding of the interdependence of independent people in our present society. Chapter Four addresses the power of spiritual awareness as a means of transcending our own personal boundaries so as to support and serve others as leaders.

Have fun discovering who you are, completing the exercise, and meeting the people in these chapters. I hope that when you complete this section, you will be excited about moving into Part Two to explore the skills you may need to acquire or develop further before making your contribution to society.

Chapter One

No Previous Experience Required

The heart can leap over barriers built by the mind.
—UNKNOWN

As we glance through the help wanted ads in our newspapers, the words "No previous experience required" are more and more a rarity. There is hardly an opportunity available today that does not require some element of experience. Yet I would wager that there is one opportunity where the requirements of passion, commitment, and caring far exceed those of experience. Of course, it is an opportunity that will never be found listed in the want ads. *That opportunity is leadership.* The call to leadership is not want ad material! You have to search for it deep within your own heart.

At some point in our lives, each of us has experienced that deep desire to make a difference, to be better than we are, to make our lives better at home or in our workplaces, to assume a leadership role in order to improve the situation for someone or some group in our communities. At the same time, we may question our abilities and wonder whether we have the knowledge, the experience, or the power to make it happen. Whatever the reason, most of us eventually find ourselves at this crossroads in our lives.

Leadership Begins with You

Most of us fear leadership, or view the possibility that we may be called upon to lead as highly improbable. So as we analyze the situations in our families, communities, or nation—or our places of employment—we lead ourselves to believe that enough feels good and looks good to satisfy us. We admit that there are some inequities and difficulties, but we rationalize these as not our responsibility. This allows us to comfortably look the other way and avoid conflict and change. Yet sooner or later our sense of justice and equity gets the better of us, and we acknowledge that this thinking may be dysfunctional. We acknowledge that our places of employment, our country, our communities, and our families have unmet needs, and someone ought to be doing something about them.

As is apt to happen in any dysfunctional situation, we look for someone or something to blame. Usually that someone is a person in a position of authority or the something is the system. In reality we all know that no single person or organization, no matter how brilliant, charismatic, or powerful, can assume the responsibility for solving all our problems. Yet when things go wrong our first response is to send up the cry, "We have no leadership! Where have all the leaders gone?" The answer to that cry is, *They haven't gone anywhere; you can see them every day, perhaps even in your own mirror!* Tom Cronin, president of Whitman College and long-time leadership educator, tells us that the single biggest factor in helping people learn to accept the responsibility to lead is "motivating or liberating [these] would-be leaders in their attitude toward themselves and toward their responsibilities to others."[1]

Consider this story of one woman's evolution from bystander to observer to leader. Betty Miller was a self-employed newspaper photographer who had come upon hard times. At age sixty-two, she suddenly found herself to be a poverty-stricken retiree living in subsidized housing in the inner city. Betty liked people, so she began to make friends with her new neighbors—street kids, gang members, homeless folks, and prostitutes. She discovered that they could not read and that much of their apparent arrogance was a cover-up for their insecurity. Betty decided to do something about it. At age sixty-eight, with only her creativity and Social Security money as resources, she created and designed "Read A Word Rummy," a card game to help nonreaders learn to read. Armed with her card game, she sat on the curbs with these new friends and began a new career of teaching literacy.

Betty subsequently founded a nonprofit corporation called Alternative Learning Programs and became a leader in the literacy movement. Her story of leadership has been aired on CBS's *60 Minutes,* and many organizations now use her material. Betty had no title and no experience as a teacher; she simply saw a problem and decided to do something about it. Her willingness to assume leadership has helped direct many convicted felons and gang members to a totally new lifestyle.

Too many people believe that leadership is a rare skill. "Nothing can be further from the truth," say Warren Bennis and Burt Nanus in *Leaders: The Strategies for Taking Charge.* "While *great* leaders may be as rare as great runners, great actors, or great painters, everyone has leadership potential, just as everyone has some ability at running, acting, and painting."[2]

Believe it or not, under the right circumstances, each of us has that innate power and ability to lead. Success in leadership is almost guaranteed to those who discover their gifts and talents and apply them to something they are passionate about. Of course we acknowledge that each of us has a great deal to learn about effective leading and leadership, but we needn't wait until we have been knighted or given a title or position before we take action. *Leadership can be thought of as a three-step process. The first step is self-knowledge, the second is self-improvement, the third is recognizing your passion and then seizing and creating opportunities to take action.* It takes vision, courage, and a will to make something happen, a desire to make a difference.

Leadership is relational; it is a process—an almost organic process. And because it is a process that cannot be fixed in time or measured precisely, no one can do it perfectly. We are all practicing.

Leadership also means leaving a mark. It means initiating and guiding and working with a group to accomplish change. Leadership is a social role—not a mere personality trait. By ideas, encouragement, and deeds, leaders show the way and influence the behavior of others. *This is leadership!*

Here's another example. A few years ago, a young New England teenager, Sarah, was deeply moved by what she experienced during a Christmas holiday visit with her mother to a domestic violence shelter. She found that there were kids just like herself at the shelter, and some were even much younger. The horror stories they shared and their keen sense of loneliness and sadness deeply moved her.

The following year, Sarah informed her family and friends that she wanted them to help her prepare for a very different holiday season, especially her birthday, which happened to fall on December 31. She asked that her traditional birthday party be held early in the month of December. Instead of the gifts she usually received, she asked her family and friends to use the money they might have spent to purchase a birthday gift for her, to purchase Christmas gifts for the kids at the domestic violence shelter. She and her family purchased and wrapped dozens of lovely gifts for these forgotten children. Of course, the story hit the newspapers and soon other families and young people in the New England area were finding their own needy populations and responding with love and generosity.

This teenager modeled the kind of leadership we need for the next century. She saw a problem and she took action! She didn't wonder why the government didn't do something for the kids. She didn't expect her parents or someone with a title and power to do something for the kids. *She did what she could to make a difference.* She organized others and inspired them to believe in her goal. She took a risk and made things happen. Others were energized by her leadership and followed her example. Did she have training or previous experience? Did she realize that she was involving herself in a process called leadership? Of course not! What she had was caring, selflessness, and desire to make a difference—and the courage to take action.

The word *leadership* means different things to different people. Some see it as connected to a title or position; others see it as the attribute of a charismatic person. In fact, it has multiple meanings and definitions. The word came into existence around the year 1800 and has been debated, discussed, and researched ever since. Let's leave the intricacies of the many theories and definitions of leadership that have evolved from this research to the theoreticians. For our purpose, I would like to make the case that *leadership is not necessarily a title or a powerful position; it is a process, it is relational, it is making something happen—it is leaving a mark.* It is an option for action that is available to every individual involved or affected by the situation at hand, as demonstrated by Betty and

Sarah. In fact, there are some who believe that in a democracy leadership is the responsibility of every citizen. If we could allow ourselves to accept this idea and believe that leaders are just ordinary citizens with a passion to make a difference, we might recognize the leader in ourselves.

Leadership begins with an individual, and then quickly spreads throughout an organization or community. When Rosa Parks refused to give up her seat on the bus, she was only one person. She certainly didn't have a title or prominent position, but she believed that segregation was wrong and she decided to do the right thing. Today, we are still feeling the effects of her courage. She had no intention of shocking the world, nor of leading a civil rights movement, but she felt so strongly about the issue that she had to act. She is an example of a courageous citizen leader. When Betty designed the card game, using her creativity and Social Security money, she had no idea of the far-reaching impact of her efforts. Her passion to help her new neighbors became a powerful source of change. Both these women were leaders, although society had not given them official titles or positions.

Preconceived Notions

Too frequently we allow ourselves to become victims of preconceived notions or of what other people think of us. This leads us to fear change, to fear failure, and to lack the will to develop our potential for leadership. We lose sight of the most important factors that lead to successful leadership: commitment, a passion to make a difference, a vision for achieving positive change, and the courage to take action. The last factor is perhaps the one that gives most of us the greatest struggle. We all dream of being successful and of making a difference but, more frequently than not, we allow ourselves to succumb to that gnawing fear of failure or ridicule that causes us to fail to take action.

Perceptions or expectations of ourselves or of others have a major influence on our success in meeting a challenge. Preconceived notions about what others may judge to be our ability to succeed or fail are deeply ingrained in our minds and hearts. Subtle messages—real or imagined—may be communicated to us all our lives. They are frequently based on where we were born and raised, the color of our skin, the socioeconomic level of our family, whether we went to college or not, which college we attended, and sometimes things as simpleminded and surprising as our gender and how we look!

If we, by our actions, continue to perpetuate the myth that only those who by someone's judgment have the right education, the right gender, the right family background, or the right skin color can ever hope to be leaders, then we will lose the opportunity to experience and learn from the vast majority of the gifted and talented people on the earth.

It is true that we have been educated to believe that only those individuals who have attained world status and visibility have the right to be called leaders. Our education also leads us to believe that only our elected officials and presidents of companies and educational institutions have the right to claim that title. But if these are the only people who can be considered leaders, then there is little room for women, minorities, and others who perform countless acts of courageous leadership every day.

The Biblical story of David and Goliath is a wonderful example of overcoming the preconceived notions of others. You may recall that everyone advised David to forget about confronting the giant. David was so little and the giant was so huge no one believed David could win. Yet David saw it from another perspective; his probable response was, "That giant is so huge, there is no way I can miss!" According to the story, little David did defeat huge Goliath. There are many lessons to be learned from this story. If we face the challenges that confront us with all our talent, knowledge, and commitment, there is no way we can miss. The preconceived notions of others can remain just that—notions.

Many of my friends are frustrated at what is happening to the political system in the United States. There are many perceived Goliaths. People we trust and elect to represent us appear to be acting on the fads and power of special interest groups that are wealthy, well organized, and for the most part out of tune with the needs of the people. My friends feel helpless and powerless in the presence of these giants. Could the situation be similar to that faced by little David? Could my friends make a difference if they put their minds to it?

The tyranny of preconceived notions and worry about what others might think reigns over many lives. This tyranny keeps us chained to limited, inflexible, cautious thinking. Overcoming these preconceived notions may take a lot of faith, but you won't discover your hidden talents until you make the decision to discard your mental roadblocks. At every opportunity, examine them, expose them, own them—and then knowingly discard them. As you gradually overcome these mental roadblocks, you will begin to think more clearly about who you are and what the possibilities are for what you wish to be. You can then envision a future in which your specific leadership contribution to society will be fulfilled. You can arrive at an understanding that you have the power to choose how to accomplish your goal of citizen leadership.

Leadership on Many Levels

The success of any group depends on many levels of leadership. This is true for families, communities, large and small organizations, public and private organizations, and, at times, for causes that are not part of an organization at all, as exhibited by the teenager in New England. Most of us have been indoctrinated by the media to believe that the charismatic person who towers above his contemporaries, enjoys extraordinary personal visibility, and leads in the grand style with a title and position is the one and only image of a true leader. Our preoccupation with this high-profile style of leadership may block our recognition of other forms of leadership and may cloud our vision of our own ability to assume responsibility as a leader.

Keep in mind that, despite the sometimes excessive media attention given to high-profile leaders, the quality of most of our lives is not solely dependent on remote leadership. We are far more dependent on leaders like Sarah who function at many levels much closer to where we live and work. The quality of our lives is improved or diminished because of our local city council members, school superintendents, plant managers, teachers, firemen, journalists, directors of social agencies, lawyers, sheriffs, hospital administrators, and so on. Our democratic society could not function if we didn't have leadership at all these levels. Our top-level leaders may set the direction, but each and every one of us must take the initiative to discover our strengths and assume responsible leadership on whatever level we may find ourselves. If we initiate and require open dialogue among all the existing levels of leadership, then every level will have a good deal to do with what goes on at every other level. This defines the characteristics of a good citizen; it also defines some of the attributes of good leadership.

Ronald Heifetz, professor of leadership at Harvard, points out that the great leaders of history and today often aid us not by what they do but rather by what they are: authority figures.[3] It is not my intent to detract from the honor these authority figures deserve. Indeed, they may provide an invaluable service at a time in history when their expertise and prominence are required. However, the daily affairs of communities and organizations throughout the world are dependent upon the leadership that can only be provided by people who are close to the problem—community leaders, family members, *ordinary people,* the Bettys and Sarahs who may be our neighbors. This is the kind of leadership that, in the depth of its caring, has discovered a passion and is determined to respond to this call to action. If you stop a moment to reflect, I am certain that you will recognize that your personal experience is filled with examples of people who have adopted the philosophy of Martin Luther King Jr.: "Everybody can be great . . . because anybody can serve. You don't have to have a college degree to serve. You don't have to make your subject and verb agree to serve. . . . You only need a heart full of grace. A soul generated by love."[4]

If we anticipate that a leadership role is beyond our ability, we will have a tendency to shy away from it or be less successful than if we put the situation in perspective. Recognizing our strengths and limitations is an important factor in making the right decision to lead or not to lead. No single person has all the answers, but you may have the answer needed at the time and place where you are now.

The extraordinary work and leadership shown by Ruth Brinker, a seventy-year-old grandmother in California, is another example of untitled leadership. This caring woman began feeding a friend who had AIDS. When he died, she found seven other victims of the disease who needed food, care, and support. This inspired her to mobilize a group of friends to respond to the needs of these seriously ill people and Project Open Hand was founded. Today, Project Open Hand feeds three thousand men, women, and children who have the HIV virus in San Francisco and Oakland, California. Ruth responded to the call for action. She became a leader in the latest stages of her life.

We are never too old or too young to assume leadership responsibility. Titles and positions may help us leverage power, but in reality the deep desire to make a difference, to have some impact on implementing positive change, is probably the most important driving force of citizen leaders.

Deciding to Act

Problems get solved when people make use of the capacities they possess. In the words of Robert F. Kennedy, "Few will have the greatness to bend history itself; but each of us can work to change a small portion of events. . . . It is from numberless diverse acts of courage and belief that human history is shaped."[5]

If we want to be treated as equal partners in an effort to effectively create a changed environment, then we must recognize our passion and have the courage to take action. If we want to be involved in the change process from the very beginning—from the point where a problem is identified and defined or a vision for the future is created—we need to step forward and be counted as active, caring citizens.

Good citizenship is our responsibility! One aspect of good citizenship is being willing to lead when our talents are needed. Progress toward a vision for the future is achieved when people make use of the strengths and knowledge they possess. I am not arguing that people in formal leadership positions should do less, but rather that all of us can and should assume the responsibility as citizen leaders to do more.[6] I want to persuade you to believe that leadership is not only a title or a powerful position; it is making something happen—it is leaving a mark! Everyone has a contribution to make, a passion to fulfill, an idea, an experience, time, specialized skills, personal contacts, wisdom, enthusiasm and so on.[7] There are rich resources to be mined if a community or organization is serious about moving forward into the twenty-first century as a healthy, energetic entity.

Leadership, then, is everyone's option and everyone's responsibility. Not everyone will contribute in the same way or at the same time. Your situation and your specific talents will determine when you will be needed to lead, and when it is your responsibility to be a supportive follower. For example, I know a dynamic woman who is an executive secretary at her place of work and a powerful leader of a youth group at her church. Another such example is a small-town podiatrist who has organized and managed an internationally known brass band. There are many examples of excellent leadership all around us.

Max DePree, former CEO of Herman Miller, the furniture manufacturing company, writes, "Everyone comes with certain gifts—but not the same gifts. True participation and enlightened leadership allow these gifts to be expressed in different ways and at different times. For the CEO to vote on the kind of drill press to buy would be foolish. For the drill press operator (who should be voting on the kind of tool to use) to vote on whether to declare a stock split would be equally foolish."[8] If everyone is willing to assume the responsibility for leadership when their specific talents are needed, then we will have better, more efficient problem solving, improved working relationships, and a growth in respect for all individuals within the organization.

If you feel the call to action—to leadership—it is your responsibility to become aware of your specific talents and of what characterizes good leadership. It is important to study and acquire sufficient knowledge of what forms the essence of leadership and how you can lead effectively. Commitment, courage, caring service, collaboration, broad inclusive visionary thinking, and a deep respect for the gifts of others are the key concepts for the new breed of leader needed for the twenty-first century.

Don't wait to be invited to lead; it probably won't happen. Don't wait until you gain more experience; it might be too late. Don't look for people with titles or positions to do it; it may not be their passion. You have the option; you have the ability; you can make a difference; you can lead and leave a mark whether it be at home, at work, in your neighborhood, community, or city—and *no experience is required!* As Goethe wrote, "Whatever you can do, or dream you can, begin it! Boldness has genius, power, and magic in it!"[9]

Chapter Two

Finding Your Voice

*Too many people overvalue what they are not and
undervalue what they are.*
—MALCOLM FORBES

Who are you? How are you unique? How do you interact with people? What do you care passionately about? Becoming rich and famous, being a leader with an impressive title or a prominent figure on television talk shows is inconsequential. What is of great consequence is to recognize that each of us does have a unique purpose in life—to somehow, at some specific time and place, make a positive leadership contribution to the world in which we live. This contribution may be at home, in your workplace, your community, or in the nation.

I can almost hear you protesting, "Come on, be real! We can't all be leaders!" With more than five billion people already on the face of the earth, it can be hard to believe in a special purpose for each and every one of our lives. It is easy to feel insignificant among the billions. But please hear me out; each of us is unique! Not only in the way we look, talk, walk, and think, but in the fact that we each bring to humanity something special that no one else can possibly offer. You bring much to the world simply because you are a human being. Add to this the richness of your relationships, family, friends, and colleagues, and the wealth of learning experiences that your life and work have brought to you, and you discover that you are both wealthy and wise. Perhaps not wealthy in the material sense, but rich in the variety of your experiences and wise in what you have learned from them. Therefore, it is important to take the time to acknowledge your natural gifts and talents, the knowledge you have acquired, the skills you have developed, and to analyze your strengths, limitations, relationships to others and inner drive. Remember, a primary aspect of leadership development is self-development, so to become a valuable citizen leader it is necessary to take the time to recognize personal strengths and to discover the purpose they bring to your life.

Passion and Purpose

Walter Turnbull discovered his purpose in an unexpected way. In *Lift Every Voice: Expecting the Most and Getting the Best from All of God's Children,* he says, "When I started the Boys Choir of Harlem 26 years ago, I did not set out to establish an internationally known performance group. I simply wanted to share the joy of music with African-American children."[1] He left his native Greenville, Mississippi, for New York City as an honors graduate of Tougaloo College with the singular dream of becoming a great opera star. To make a living while working toward his goal, he taught music for twelve years in New York City's public schools. In 1968, he also began working with a small church choir of African American boys. The boys, ages eight to eighteen, came from across Harlem, the uppermost tip of Manhattan. Most of them came from single-parent, poor families living in an environment of crime and drugs. Turnbull saw the discipline and structure of the choir as a positive alternative to the streets for these inner-city children.[2]

Turnbull passionately threw himself into working with these boys. In 1975, the group was incorporated as the Boys Choir of Harlem.[3] His leadership, energy, and love for the boys have moved this group to world-renowned success. Today they have performed across the United States and have made eight European tours and three Asian tours. They have appeared on television, including CBS's *60 Minutes,* and have sung with Luciano Pavarotti and Kathleen Battle. They even sang at President Clinton's inauguration.[4]

Indeed, Walter Turnbull literally found his voice! In addition to his work as director of the choir, he has sung with many prominent opera groups and gives annual recitals in New York City.[5] He has not only accomplished his dream to become a great singer, but he has also discovered his role as a leader in the lives of hundreds of young men who might have become involved in crime, drugs, and the violence of the streets of New York.

As we begin the journey on the path to leadership, it is important to first believe in ourselves and know that we have the potential to lead. Turnbull knew that he had the potential to become a great singer; his skill in working with young people was a gift he discovered in the process of his own development. Some important prerequisites to effective leadership are: understanding our gifts, talents, strengths, limitations, and what we care deeply about; developing the desire to lead; and then accepting the fact that leadership means taking action.

Sometimes leadership is described as an art—a performing art that takes continuous study and practice. Max DePree does a masterful job of addressing this. He states, "Leadership is an art, something to be learned over time, not simply by reading books. Leadership is more tribal than scientific, more a weaving of relationships than an amassing of information, and, in that sense, I don't know how to pin it down in every detail."[6]

Describing leadership as an art releases us from imposing narrow, fixed definitions on the process. It is continuously evolving. Most performing artists will readily admit that they never completely master the intricacies of their chosen instrument. It is a lifetime endeavor. Try to imagine that the instrument in this performing art of leadership is *yourself*. To master this specific instrument, we must each learn as much as possible about ourselves. I think of this as a process of finding your voice. Every human voice has a distinctive timbre and quality, which can artfully blend with others to produce a rich, vibrant sound. Likewise, one important aspect of the essence of leadership is forming rich, productive relationships that produce healthy communities, families, and organizations. Therefore, in addition to understanding ourselves, it is important to learn all we can about the skills and concepts involved in the process of leadership. Ultimately, leadership development is a continuing process or art of self-development and understanding. Like a performing art, it takes many, many hours of study and practice! It is a demanding process that requires being open to an inner voice, being able to accept and integrate feedback from others, and staying open to new experiences and information. Yes, there is a great deal to learn about the instrument of ourselves, about leading and leadership.

Marika Critelli is now in her late teens, but she has been running a recycling business since she was in the sixth grade. Let's take a look at what this has to do with the ongoing process of her development as a young leader. Marika had been raised in an environmentally conscious family. When she was in the sixth grade, she decided that she needed a job so as to make some extra spending money. At this same point, she participated in a summer camp where the seriousness of environmental issues had been discussed. Reinforced by her family interests and the events at the camp, she became quite well versed on the topic and wanted to do something positive about the problem. Her dad suggested that she think about a recycling business because this would give her the opportunity to take the lead in helping others improve the environment, as well as let her make some money.

Although Marika was apprehensive about a kid starting a business and attempting to teach adults the importance of environmental issues, her passion for the cause moved her to action. She had many ups and downs along the way, but today the business is thriving. In addition, Marika has learned a great deal about being a citizen leader for a cause about which she feels passionately. She has learned the value of being well organized, the need to take risks, the importance of understanding the needs and values of others, and the importance of setting achievable goals. These are valuable leadership lessons. She has also educated many people about the problems of waste in our environment, and convinced them to become involved. Marika says, "If you're going to be a citizen leader, you've got to have a lot of courage, and passionately believe in what you're doing."

Marika believes that both now and in the future, her leadership will be expressed through education and action. In fact, she says she has made "education and action" her motto. Marika has been fortunate to find her voice at a very early age. Whatever she does in the future, the leadership lessons she learned about risk taking, communication, decision making, humor, and ethics running this business will certainly help her become a better person and leader. Marika is a very young citizen who decided that she could make a difference. Her youth and lack of experience could have been obstacles, but with her parents' encouragement and her concern for the environment, she took action. *This is leadership!*

There are many skills and qualities that we admire in others whom we recognize as effective leaders. I have often heard people say, "I can't tell you what leadership is, but I know it when I see it." People who worked with Marika probably said, "There goes a young leader." Marika and Turnbull revealed different sets of strengths and attributes although both exhibited strong leadership. You will readily agree that every single one of us has a distinctive set of strengths and limitations. Knowing and understanding this are the first steps in the process of self-development. For years, leadership scholars have carried on heated debates about the beneficial attributes of leadership. In the end, it is acknowledged that no two successful leaders manifest the same set! Much depends upon the situation or organization. However, knowing and understanding yourself appear to be the keys to finding your voice.

Self-Awareness and Self-Confidence

In *Taking Charge,* Perry Smith tells us, "Leaders should think of themselves as individuals surrounded by mirrors of many kinds."[7] Only a few of these mirrors give the leader an accurate reflection of himself or herself. "Even the most consistent of leaders is many things to many people."[8]

Smith tells us that leaders must realize that they are five people: who they think they are; who they are perceived to be by their subordinates, peers, and superiors; and who they really are. He goes on to say that in many cases, there is a close relationship among these different perceptions. However, at other times the relationships are not close at all! The quest for leadership is primarily an inner journey to discover our true selves, which include our strengths, skills, prejudices, and talents, and a recognition of our unique gifts and some of our limitations. This inner adventure can also lead us to a better understanding of what we really care about. Our actions will then be filled with energy, caring, and commitment because we will have discovered our purpose and passion.

As a young person, I never gave much thought to leading or leadership. I grew up an inner-city Chicago kid in a hard-working, blue-collar neighborhood. Although no one in my immediate family held official positions of power or leadership, I was taught that I could become anything that I dreamed about; I just had to study, work hard, and be responsible, and it could happen. With that kind of encouragement from my family, I usually accepted difficulties as just another challenge, and frequently found myself in positions of leadership. As a young adult, I was happiest and most satisfied in situations that required organizing and energizing a group of people to work toward a goal or vision.

It wasn't until many years later, as I found myself in formal leadership positions and began the study of leadership, that I looked back upon those years and recognized the many forces of love and encouragement that had assisted me in the process of finding my voice, my passion. Yes, my passion has been and is working with people as a teacher, mentor, and motivator. However, I learned that discovering what you care passionately about is only the first step in leadership development. Being open to further learning and possessing a willingness to take action will determine whether you have really found your voice.

Frequently in my early adult years, I had to deal with failure and rejection because I pushed people too hard instead of gently encouraging them toward their goals. Although this was sometimes discouraging, there were several key people, mentors, who helped me understand myself, my strengths, and my limitations. They were willing to encourage me when I failed, applaud my successes, point out my weaknesses, and help me understand that life is a continuous process of learning. Perhaps their most important contribution to my development was their consistent reinforcement of the concept that I had been given many gifts and opportunities that were meant to be shared with others. Such mentors are invaluable!

My passion has been and is to creatively teach and help build the self-confidence of people—especially young people. I am energized by interacting with people who have a desire to learn. It brings me great satisfaction to help them understand that they have the option to lead and the ability to play an important part in designing their future. It took me many years to discover my voice—my passion—and many more to learn to use it effectively. I still have a great deal to learn. Amazingly, the more I learn, the more I realize I don't know! However, I am convinced that the role of citizen leader is everyone's option and everyone's responsibility. Every community, every family, every organization would benefit tremendously if each of us took full responsibility and used our talents for creating or implementing positive change. This requires self-confidence.

Self-confidence can be defined as an awareness of and faith in our own capabilities and a knowledge of our limitations. Through self-awareness comes the confidence needed to lead and to form strong teams of people to accomplish a common vision for the community, organization, or group in which we are involved. Our capabilities become clear and strong and far outweigh our limitations only when we are willing to work to identify and develop them.

Objective Introspection

Perhaps the greatest benefit a leader gains from such objective introspection is improved performance. Leaders who know who they really are generally outperform leaders who are unwilling to admit imperfection. Introspective leaders can avoid serious mistakes and can project a sense of self-awareness and self-confidence that gains the respect and support of their colleagues and others with whom they are involved. This self-awareness and self-confidence also help the individual understand when to relinquish the leadership role and assume the role of supportive and committed follower.

A few years ago, a group of young professionals in a leadership development program were involved in a weeklong Outward Bound experience. One of the exercises demanded the use of a compass for the team to successfully maneuver their way through mountainous terrain toward a specific goal. A member of the team happened to have spent many years in the military; he had frequently participated in similar exercises. Naturally, he quickly gained the confidence of the group and with their approval assumed the role of leader. Many hours later, the tired group finally found their way through the wilderness to the base camp. They had walked several miles in the wrong direction! There was a great deal of teasing, joking, and blame by the group. The good-humored acceptance of the teasing and the humble apology of the team leader were powerful lessons for everyone involved. This exercise taught the group that:

- No matter how experienced and proficient one might be, there is always a risk of failure.
- Humility and willingness to admit an error can serve to strengthen the trust and commitment of a group.
- Sometimes collaborative problem solving is far more effective than counting on one person to have all the answers.

Honest answers to introspective questions, through the assistance of those who work with and for us, can help leaders avoid becoming out of touch, domineering, or irrelevant. Knowing your ideals and what your intellectual, psychological, stylistic, and spiritual strengths and limitations are can improve your ability to provide enlightened leadership and energy to an organization, community, or family.

Honest answers can also improve your understanding of others and build your skills to mobilize other people's energies toward accomplishing a common goal. While scholars may disagree on the theories or attributes of leadership, there is a strong consensus that leaders must be interpersonally competent. A leader must be able to listen, take advice, lose arguments—and *be prepared to follow* when it is apparent that the situation demands the skills possessed by someone else. Only a very self-aware, self-assured person with a strong belief in the power of every individual to be a leader can do this. Unless a leader can develop the trust and respect of others by exhibiting a humble self-confidence born through self-awareness and by acknowledging the insights and competence of others, the leader will be ineffective.

Warren Bennis, a noted leadership scholar, did an extensive study of twenty-nine successful business persons. In *On Becoming a Leader,* he emphatically pointed out that an essential part of a leader's success and integrity is his or her willingness to accept the challenge of developing personal knowledge. Bennis wrote, "To become a leader, then, you must become yourself, become the maker of your own life."[9] He also noted that self-knowledge is "the most difficult task any of us faces. But until you truly know yourself, strengths and weaknesses, know what you want to do and why you want to do it, you cannot succeed in any but the most superficial sense of the word."[10]

John Gardner, former Secretary of Health, Education and Welfare and prolific writer about leadership and community, has stated that there are four moral goals of leadership:

- Releasing human potential
- Balancing the needs of the individual and the community
- Defending the fundamental values of community
- Instilling in individuals a sense of initiative and responsibility[11]

Leaders who make every attempt to acquire an in-depth knowledge of who they really are will also make every attempt to cultivate leadership in others and rise above petty self-interest. They will be responsible for releasing new human potential, which will help make organizations, communities, and society far better places to live and work. In Chapter Ten, we'll spend more time discussing power and relationships.

It has been said that visionary leaders take us to places we have never been before—but there are no blueprints to these unknown places of the future! Before a leader attempts to step out into the uncharted territory of the twenty-first century, it would be wise to determine what assets he or she has and what team members need to be cultivated to begin the exploration of this unknown territory.

As John Gardner writes, "Human beings have always employed an enormous variety of clever devices for running away from themselves. . . . We can keep ourselves so busy, fill our lives with so many diversions, stuff our heads with so much knowledge, involve ourselves with so many people and cover so much ground that we never have time to probe the fearful and wonderful world within. . . . By middle life most of us are accomplished fugitives from ourselves."[12]

To harness the power that can evolve when you know yourself, you must discover and acknowledge where your passion lies. Try the exercise presented in Exhibit 2.1, and see if it helps you arrive at a somewhat better understanding of yourself.

More important than this simple exercise is the power that can evolve when we grow in knowledge, comfort, and acceptance of the gifts and limitations that make up who we really are. Remember— accepting who you really are, discovering your passion, and finding

Exhibit 2.1. What Is Most Important to You?

1. Using the spaces provided in column A, make a list of ten issues that you care deeply about. They can be social issues, family issues, work issues, or national issues. The only determining factor is that you care deeply about them.
2. After you have created your list, rank the issues (assigning numbers 1–10 in the spaces provided) according to the depth of your feeling for each of them.
3. Now select two of these issues that you can choose to do something about within the next two or three months, and list them in column B.
4. Which one of these two is most important to you? Once you have made your decision, list that issue in column C.

Rank	A	B	C
____	_____	_____	_____
____	_____	_____	
____	_____		
____	_____		
____	_____		
____	_____		
____	_____		
____	_____		
____	_____		
____	_____		

5. Commit yourself to taking steps toward addressing the issue in column C. You will be asked to outline a plan of action in Chapter Thirteen.

your voice take time and reflection. A vision or mission doesn't just reveal itself in a flash of light or a brilliant dream! It evolves from knowledge of ourselves, our values, and our desires. To successfully achieve this vision, we need to take what we know about ourselves and our relationships to others and apply this knowledge to a plan of action with commitment and purpose. We need to instill in others a sense of initiative and responsibility. In the words of Lao-tzu,

> To know how other people behave takes intelligence,
> but to know myself takes wisdom.
> To manage other people's lives takes strength,
> but to manage my own life takes true power.[13]

Further insights into opportunities for self-development can be found in the Resources section at the end of the book. Leadership development programs, books, and videos can all help you in your search for deeper knowledge of yourself and your passions.

Chapter Three

The Two Sides of Leadership

If the United States is faltering now, it is because of a
failure of followership more than a failure of leadership.
—ROBERT E. KELLEY

We've spent the last two chapters talking about the importance of knowing ourselves and our passion so as to generate the creativity and self-confidence necessary to assume a leadership role. It is of equal importance for us to understand that loyal, creative, energetic *followership* is also a crucial role in the success of any enterprise. As we continue this discussion of the vital role of citizens as leaders, we would be remiss if we did not spend some time studying and recognizing the essentially seamless nature of leadership and followership.

Leadership and Followership: A Symbiotic Relationship

We all appreciate being recognized as the leader when our unique strength is needed. It is also important to learn to energetically support another person's leadership when a different strength is required. For example, you may be the construction or design engineer on a building project, but if someone is injured on the job you immediately rely on the wisdom, leadership, and expertise of a health expert to respond to the emergency. Or, you may chair a board of education, but you understand that you and the other board members need to rely on the expertise and knowledge of the principal and teachers to make high-quality educational policy decisions. Leadership and followership have a symbiotic relationship. Science teaches us that, in symbiosis, two or more very dissimilar organisms form a relationship in which each depends on the other. So it is with leadership and followership. Leaders should nurture strong, loyal followers who can be depended on and who can assume the lead if called upon to do so. Followers need to support and encourage their leader to successfully achieve their common goal.

This new paradigm, depicting a highly interactive, interdependent society, is coming at us from all sides. Journalists, reporters, and authors from every sector are delivering the message of a need for collaboration. Television, the press, movies, and personal development programs are all incorporating and popularizing this concept of interdependence and interaction. In this type of complex, highly interactive environment, one must learn to move from leadership to followership or followership to leadership with grace and energy.

In much of the past leadership literature, a prevailing notion has been that the leader is a savior and that the role of the follower is a passive one. To our disadvantage, even some of our most current literature leads us to view a leader as a single powerful person at the top of a hierarchical chart. In this context, it is the responsibility of the leader to point a group of somewhat passive followers toward the direction that will take them to success. This idea is very troublesome because it implies that a single leader at the top knows all, can do all, and will lead us to success. By implication, this tells us that our only choice is to follow submissively. This narrow view places unrealistic demands on our leaders and deeply undermines the talent and confidence of the rest of us.

Let's try to open our minds to a new view of leadership that incorporates followers as active, responsible participants in achieving mutually agreed-upon goals. The key phrase here is *mutually agreed-upon* goals. In this model, leaders and followers together choose a direction or plan. The leader may then set the pace, but the unique gifts of the team members are recognized and followers are encouraged to be creative in designing a means of achieving the goal. Therefore, there are times when those who were followers become leaders and leaders become loyal followers. This implies that there can be no leader without followers and that followers need the opportunity to collaborate in the development of a unified vision. It also implies that followers should be encouraged to exhibit their talents in accomplishing the vision.

In *Leadership Jazz,* Max DePree gives us an excellent metaphor for this new view. He tells us that the jazz-band leader must choose the music, find musicians with the right talents, and then perform for the public. Obviously, the effect of the performance does not solely rest on the shoulders of the band leader. He may have the power to decide what to play and to set the pace; but success depends upon the talent of the individual musicians, their ability to perform as a group, the quality of their improvisations, the environment, the response of the audience, and many other hidden factors.[1] Each musician must exhibit both leadership skills and followership skills in the same performance. What a perfect example of the seamless nature of leadership and followership!

We must constantly remind ourselves that both roles are crucial to the success of any enterprise, at work, in the community, or at home. Leadership is a *function,* not a title or a status; therefore there may be times when it is necessary for a person who has been functioning as a leader to function as a follower. To understand this is to recognize the interdependent nature of leadership and followership. Leaders and followers influence and empower each other. One cannot exist without the other anymore than a sheet of paper can have only one side! Bryson and Crosby, prominent leadership scholars, tell us, "In a world where shared power is more effective than individual power, the tasks of leadership must be widely shared. No one person can embody all the needed qualities or perform all the tasks. People will also pass into and out of leadership roles; a person may be a leader on one issue and a follower on others. This year's leader on a particular issue may even be next year's follower on that same issue."[2] Knowing yourself, your strengths, and your limitations—as stressed in our earlier discussions—is extremely useful in helping you decide when to take the lead and when to be a loyal, supportive follower. In either case, this new point of view encourages you to think of yourself as a partner in a mutual, interactive process and not as a solo act. If your actions reflect this thinking, you can eliminate the polarized leader-follower tensions so frequently exhibited in organizations and communities.

An acquaintance of mine, Diane, shared the great difficulty she had in giving up her position as head of the board of a nonprofit organization. She found herself constantly comparing her leadership style with that of her successor. Even though she did not verbalize her comparisons, her attitude caused increased tension with the new chairperson and discomfort among other board members. Her nonverbal communication indicated that she expected the new leader to continue doing things as they had been done. The personal tension she felt ultimately led her to disconnect from the organization altogether. The organization lost a faithful supporter and Diane lost the opportunity to learn new ways of doing things.

Diane claimed that she had never had the opportunity to learn the value of being a loyal, supportive follower. It is true that there is no organized system of feedback and performance evaluation for most volunteers who dedicate time and energy to nonprofit organizations. So when a job had to be done, Diane did it herself. She failed to delegate, she failed to recognize the unique gifts of the people on her teams. She was impatient. This sometimes meant long hours and hard work alone. This also led to her single-minded view of how things needed to be done. Now her advice to other citizen leaders is, present your point of view, learn to listen to others, be open to other styles of leadership, and remember that loyal, supportive followership is the other side of the coin of good leadership.

Some of the most difficult concepts to embrace are that leadership and followership are seamless processes; that the relationship of leader and follower is symbiotic; that each role benefits greatly through the interdependent nature of the relationship; that the leader today may be the follower tomorrow. Our society places so much emphasis on leadership as a status, a title, or a position, that it is difficult for us to understand the power that evolves from the acceptance of the essential nature of both roles.

Styles of Followership

Just as there is effective and ineffective leadership, there is also acceptable and unacceptable followership. I have personally experienced three basic styles of followership. The first I will designate as *docile sheep*. These individuals never question an activity or order.

They never offer a suggestion for a better way to accomplish a task. They seem to lack energy, appear apathetic, and simply move along with the crowd because everyone is going in that direction. They rarely display any creativity and would panic if they were asked to take charge or were given the freedom to choose a direction. They prefer to play it safe and place unmanageable burdens of solo decision making and direction setting upon their leaders. This style of followership can be self-inflicted or can be superimposed by the culture of the organization or community. If the organization clearly implies that challenges to the status quo are unacceptable, then sheeplike followership will be the dominant style exhibited. If individuals lack self-confidence and have never had the encouragement or mentoring to help them recognize their strengths and limitations, they may find that they are most comfortable when there are others to tell them what to do.

A second style of followership might be termed *passive-aggressive*. This style of followership is tenuous at best. These individuals submit to the leader's requests and goals only because they fear the loss of position, the loss of the favor of the leader, or public embarrassment. They grudgingly carry out orders and carefully hide their lack of enthusiasm and loyalty toward the leader behind a "yes sir" or "yes ma'am" facade. The problem with this style of followership is that it is like a shadow—it is with you in the light, but gone at night! Beware of this style of followership. Leaders who do not encourage and search for the talent among their followers may find themselves surrounded by these fearful, disloyal followers. As long as the leader is successful and appears to be in power, the followers submit to all requests. At the first sign of difficulty, weakness, failure, or loss of power on the part of the leader, these followers disappear. They voice public disagreement with the policies and plans of the leader and ultimately bring the organization or community to a state of chaos, making it a hotbed of discontent.

The implication here is that if a leader recognizes the existence of these two styles of followership, steps should be taken to encourage those with whom they work to express differences of opinion without fear of retribution, to offer suggestions for new and different ways of doing things, and to be willing to take charge even if the situation looks difficult. A leader who understands the value of active, supportive followership will share power, listen carefully to the ideas of all members of the team, and applaud calculated risk taking—even if it sometimes ends in failure. The followers will then recognize that the leader perceives and respects the talents found in the group and is willing to share the lead when the opportunity for new and different talent presents itself. This interactive atmosphere supports creativity.

If, as sometimes occurs, every effort of the leader to contribute encouragement and support is disregarded by a passive-aggressive team member, then it is the leader's responsibility to sever the relationship. Dismissing someone from an organization may be one of the most difficult decisions a leader must make. But if all avenues have been tried and the individual continues to seed discontent and chaos, it is the responsibility of the leader to act for the good of the organization as well as of the other members of the team involved.

The third and most effective form of followership is a *totally involved, loyal, supportive followership*. These individuals have been included in the designing of the future of the organization or community and see themselves as both leaders and followers. They know that their talents are recognized. They participate with energy, intelligence, and self-confidence without the need or promise of being made a star player. They are interactively involved in the future of the organization or community and view themselves as key to its success. They are brought together by their individual decisions to make their personal dream a part of the institutional dream and a determination to make that dream a reality.

Leaders and Followers Determine Each Other's Success

Arnold Fletcher, a concert pianist and former academic leader, has frequently found himself in the role of both a leader and a follower. He is an excellent example of someone who understands the value of both roles. He has served as president of a college and then served in a follower position at the same institution. He has moved from the position of leader to follower and follower to leader with grace and energy! He is now a resident of a life-care community and, once again, finds himself in both leadership and followership positions. He is seventy-seven years young, energetic, and active; he still participates in concerts and recitals and serves as vice president of the residential governance organization. Arnold indicates that the official leaders of this new type of community must consistently be reminded about who their constituents are. They must be sensitive to the residents, not because of their age, but because these people bring varied backgrounds, wisdom, and many years of positional and nonpositional leadership experience to the community. Most of the residents, like Arnold and his wife, Toni, want to play a role in shaping their community. They are supportive followers but also have lifelong leadership experiences to contribute. They wish to be actively involved in the way their community operates. They have a good understanding of the responsibilities of both leaders and followers. They recognize the need for others to assume a leadership role in the lifestyle they have chosen; however, they want to be included, at least in an advisory capacity, in the decision-making processes.

In addition, Arnold stresses that the residents must frequently be reminded that loyal, supportive followership is essential to make their community a high-quality place to live. Active followership places different demands on leadership, and leaders in life-care communities must acknowledge that the residents are not a blank slate for them to write on. A primary demand in this situation, and most others, is open, regular communication and recognition of the unique contributions of each individual.

The relative roles of leaders and followers in determining goals will always vary from group to group. Nevertheless, the recognition of the symbiotic relationship of leadership and followership leads to respect, trust, confidence, and an understanding that both roles are vital and that all of us will find ourselves in the role of leader and follower many times in a day, a week, a month, or a year.

Joe Rost, in *Leadership for the Twenty-First Century*, tells us that "followers and leaders develop a relationship wherein they influence one another as well as the organization and society, and that is leadership. They do not do the same things in the relationship, just as the composers and musicians do not do the same thing in making music, but they are both essential to leadership."[3] This metaphor clearly indicates the value of the intimate cooperation of sometimes very dissimilar partners. As with the jazz band, we can carry this example one step further and view the seamlessness of leadership and followership in the functions of the musicians who make up an orchestra. An orchestra is composed of a great variety of musicians who each spend many hours learning to blend the sounds of their diverse instruments to create beautiful music that is pleasing to the ear of the audience. First, the musicians must be talented people who know how to produce quality music with their specific instruments. Then they must learn to operate as a team—working together to create the sound as conceived by the composer. In making this happen, various members of the orchestra will assume different roles—sometimes they will lead as a soloist and at others they will follow, offering strong, supportive background music while a colleague becomes the lead soloist. To produce the energy and beauty of the music as designed by the composer, both roles must be assumed with dignity, creativity, attention, and dedication. Moving between the roles of leadership and followership in the context of an orchestra, as in an organization or community, should be a seamless and fluid process.

Ultimately, followers can determine the success of a leader. Remember that most successful organizations thrive on the commitment and enthusiasm of dedicated followers, not on the words of an employment contract. Leaders and followers working together, recognizing when to lead and when to follow and complementing each other's strengths, are the team that make a vision real. Followers should all reflect on the power they confer upon the leader to act, and recognize that their roles are interdependent and fluid. Without supportive followers, a leader will ultimately fail.

Every day can be a new learning and growth experience if we respect the gifts and unique talents of those with whom we live and work. If we are attentive, we can even learn some very profound lessons about leadership and followership from the living things that surround us. For example, Angeles Arrien recounted the following commentary, based on the work of Milton Olson, in a speech at the 1991 Organizational Development Network titled "Lessons from Geese."

• As geese fly, the flapping of their wings creates an uplift for the birds that follow. By flying in a "V" formation, each bird gains a 71 percent greater flying range.

Lesson: People who share a common goal can get where they are going more quickly and easily when they rely on each other's support and strength.

• A goose that falls out of formation feels the drag and resistance of flying alone. It quickly moves back into formation to gain the benefit of the lifting power of the bird in front of it.

Lesson: If we had as much sense as a goose, we would work with others who are headed where we want to go. Getting there will be easier if we are willing to accept their help and give our help in return.

•   When the lead goose tires, it moves back to a position where it gets the benefit of the lift and allows another goose to take the lead.

Lesson: It pays to share leadership. People who are interdependent and recognize each other's skills, strengths, and unique gifts have greater opportunity of reaching their goals. Sharing the power of leadership ensures the opportunity for everyone to contribute to the desired outcome.

•   The geese flying in formation honk to encourage those up front to keep up the good work.

Lesson: Productivity is much greater in groups where there is encouragement. Leaders need to be encouraged by their followers and followers need the encouragement of their leaders. Encouragement, enthusiasm, and humor help eliminate the stress that accompanies high productivity.

•   When a goose gets sick or wounded, two geese drop out of formation and follow it down to help and protect it. They stay with it until it dies or is able to fly again. Then they launch out with another formation or catch up with their original flock.

Lesson: If we have as much sense as geese, we will stand by each other in difficult times as well as when we are strong.

Mother Nature can teach us many profound lessons if we pay attention to her! Remember, *today you lead; tomorrow you follow!*

Chapter Four

Use Your Internal Compass

*The journey of spiritual growth requires courage and
initiative and independence of thought and action.*
—M. SCOTT PECK

In Chapter Three, we spoke about followership and leadership as
seamless processes, each being totally dependent on the other. If we
accept this premise and are willing to give 100 percent of our energies whether we are functioning as leader or as follower, then we
have formed a true partnership. According to Robert Kelley, noted
author and scholar of leadership, "In true partnerships, competent
people join together to achieve what they could not achieve alone."[1]
To function as a true partner also takes *inner strength,* self-knowledge,
integrity, excellent relational skills, and an understanding of leadership as service. Inner strength—what is it? How do we achieve it?
Are we born with it? Would an hour of exercise daily help us to
achieve it?

The Spiritual Side of Leadership

No, we certainly aren't born with inner strength; physical exercise
might help by relieving stress, but the exercise of personal intellectual discipline is the most useful means of achieving it. Inner
strength is developed by striving for an understanding of the relationship of our spirituality, our values, and our external behavior. If
our external behavior reflects our spirituality (inner strength) and
values, then we can say we are at peace with ourselves and are

maintaining a balanced perspective. The appeal of a spiritual side of leadership becomes more clear if you stand it against the backdrop of larger social trends. For one thing, talk of spirituality and even of religion is no longer taboo. The combination of spirituality, service, and action is frequently spoken of as *servant leadership*. The remarkable growth of the Robert K. Greenleaf Center for Servant-Leadership in Indianapolis, Indiana, is a sign of the growing interest in the spiritual dimension of leadership in our lives and our work.

Robert K. Greenleaf, a former management researcher at AT&T, is credited with introducing the idea of servant leadership into the vocabulary of leadership educators and into the workplace. His philosophy is built on the premise that the leader exists primarily to serve a group of followers; they grant the leader their allegiance in response to a willingness to include and serve them in achieving mutually established goals. Greenleaf's philosophy is deeply spiritual, yet it is finding a home in the secular work of corporations, nonprofit organizations, and educational institutions. It appears to have slowly emerged as a concept that helps us cope with the stress and insecurity of the nineties.[2] An article in *Training* magazine indicates that servant leadership promotes "service to others, a holistic approach to work, personal development and shared decision making—characteristics that place it squarely in the mainstream of conventional talk about empowerment, total quality and participative management."[3]

The social trends of corporate downsizing, economic insecurity, the global marketplace, the rising crime rate, the breakdown of the family, and the increasing distrust of all leadership are persuading many people to search for a spiritual connection. There is a growing belief that these trends demand an energy that can only be derived from the development of inner strength or spiritual awareness. Some believe that an understanding of the place of spirituality in our lives is the only thing that can sustain us through the fundamental dilemmas of leadership as we move rapidly toward the next century.

Spirituality is being recognized as a very important component of leadership. Some of you may disagree with this statement, perhaps because of a preconceived notion that to speak about spirituality means to embark on a discussion of religion. That is certainly not my intention. When I use the word spirit or spirituality, I am referring to an inner strength, a sense of balance and depth. Religion is a support structure, a tool, an external symbol that some of us may use to help us understand our spirituality. However, my premise when discussing spirituality is in harmony with that of Greenleaf. That is, effective leadership should be based on integrity, honesty, love, and respect for all humanity—with service as the primary motivation for the action. This is a deeply spiritual approach to leadership. This is also in agreement with another leadership author, James A. Ritscher, who says that "spirituality is an *experience of depth in life;* it is living life with heart" rather than merely concentrating on superficial externals.[4] For some, spirituality involves the belief in a god. For others, it takes a different form. "Spirituality is the awareness that there is something more to life than just [a] narrow, ego-oriented view" of the world.[5]

A Sense of Balance

Our culture tends to externalize everything. A discussion about spirituality automatically reverts to a church, an organization, or a religious denomination. Although all these may be excellent resources, they are all external symbols of our support systems. Our culture also describes the good life or the good leader as someone who can skillfully manipulate external arrangements. Little or no attention is given to spirituality, the need to center and strengthen inner well-being and to maintain a sense of balance so as to effectively and ethically make an impact on our environment. However, good leadership education is not simply about the skills necessary to manipulate the external world. It is about the personal discipline of the inner self as well. We must possess that inner strength before we can transcend our own personal boundaries to support and serve others. I am convinced that the combination of inner strength and effective leadership skills is a necessity for the individual striving to lead in a time of rapid change and chaos.

Even well-established leadership development programs are acknowledging a need to introduce the concept of the value of developing inner strength in their training programs. "'There is a sacred aspect to good leadership training,' muses Randall White, director of specialized client applications at the Center for Creative Leadership (CCL) in Greensboro, North Carolina. 'We talk about the idea of becoming committed to being a better person, and treating others as you'd want to be treated. For years, we've been talking about flipping over the organizational pyramid and serving all the people.' In leadership training, and in the most progressive organizations, he says, the emphasis has shifted from looking at knowledge, skills and behaviors to examining values, attitudes and beliefs."[6]

Our everyday world of family and work is filled with activity. A discussion of spirituality appears to fly in the face of this reality. When faced with the issue, our immediate reaction is to question it. It is difficult to believe that we can have both at the same time: a world of work and action, and a deep sense of spirituality or centeredness. But that is because we define loud voices, intense time schedules, and long hours as action, and silence, prayer, and meditation as spirituality. These are very limiting definitions. With this mind-set, we can easily allow ourselves to be drawn into an either-or situation that may evolve to a state of confusion and lost energy. Must the two be thought of as distinct and separate ways of life? I don't believe so. In today's competitive world, it is important to maintain a strong sense of values, of centeredness, of balance—for our own personal well-being as well as for the well-being of the organization or community we are leading. A person who understands this will make every attempt to maintain a dynamic tension between the external and internal forces that govern life—the internal forces being recognized as spirituality and the external forces as actions reflecting values and internal strength. Achieving this balance is not easy, but it is the best way to avoid burnout and poor health. Those of us who believe in a higher power recognize that our spiritual growth in a world of constant turmoil is guided by an invisible hand with infinitely greater wisdom than that of which our unaided thinking and will are capable. This invisible hand might be compared to the needle of a compass.

Being an avid camper, I find long walks in the woods, the smell of campfires, and the music of the birds very refreshing after a stressful period at work. Hiking, canoeing, and absorbing the sounds of nature are my therapy; they inspire my creativity! They help me maintain a sense of balance. Anyone who likes to hike or canoe knows and understands the value and necessity of owning a compass. No matter how turned around you might find yourself in a dense, quiet forest, or how completely disoriented by the violence of a sudden storm on a lake, the compass needle will always point north. A good compass is a true and steady companion to the lover of the out-of-doors.

On one occasion, some friends and I were caught in an unpredicted storm on a Boundary Waters lake in northern Minnesota. As the storm subsided and we began to relax from our battle with the water, we found ourselves completely turned around, confused, tired, soaked to the skin, and lost! We discovered that the shoreline looked the same in every direction. Deciding what direction we should take to get us back to our campsite could have been a very difficult task. However, we had what we needed to help us make the right decision. We pulled out our waterproof compass and found that the winds had turned us completely around and we were headed in the exact opposite direction, away from our original destination. We didn't know how far off course we were, but the needle of the compass was strong and steady—still pointing north! It served as our guide to correct our position and begin our trek back to the campsite. It was at that point that I began to understand the concept of *centeredness,* of maintaining a balance of spirituality and action in my life. Whether we glided in calm waters or exerted all our energies to control the canoe in the wild action of the storm, the needle was always centered; it pointed north.

Aha, I said to myself. That is how I should maintain my life! Whether conditions are wild and changing or calm and orderly, I should have a strong sense of my values and spirituality or centeredness to help me face the external challenges each day may bring.

This centeredness helps us to make the right decisions on our journey through life. If we can manage to think of the balanced life as the readout of our internal compass, we might be able to understand the value of the integration of our spiritual and active lives. *Balance* is what we want to achieve. Our external actions should reflect people in touch with who they really are; people who believe in high productivity but who also maintain strong values and inner strength. We should strive to deliberately and purposefully strengthen our spirituality as well as our interpersonal and leadership skills. Together they can serve as the essence of who we are, which in turn makes a constructive life a possibility. If we choose to use our energies to develop only our external performance, we will probably soon find that something is missing.

Something Missing

Katherine Tyler Scott tells us that "most leaders feel ill prepared for the responsibilities that are expected of them. Many lack a clear sense of their motivations for serving and leading. They know they are expected to be leaders in their organizations . . . [or communities], but there is a limited understanding of why this is important."[7] They are frequently heard saying, "Something is missing."[8]

Scott says that when she pursues the comment, "something is missing," she discovers very quickly that what people are missing in this frenzy of activity is *meaning*. "They are seeking connections and connectedness between what they do and who they are. . . . Their preparation for leadership has lacked opportunities for in-depth reflection on . . . [who they are] and their relationship to the external."[9] Scott believes this nurturance of spirit is what is missing.

Is there something missing for you? Our external behavior is usually a reflection of our spirituality, our sense of balance or the lack of it. It is a clear sign of who we are and of the kind of world we want to create. Our actions are the visible expression of our inner selves, of how well we keep our eye on that internal compass. Our inner strength is the sustaining force that holds us together when we find ourselves in difficult situations. It is the support we need when we know that a decision we are about to make may be very unpopular. It is a means by which we keep before us that faith, religious belief, or sense of values that guides us when we are about to take action in the world of practical affairs. It is the voice of our conscience that keeps us honest when the urge to take the easy way out presents itself.

If we choose to plunge our energies into external action alone, with no attempt to nurture our inner core, our spirituality, we tend to develop a habit of frenetic activity. We may find ourselves falling into a pattern that attempts to control everything and everyone around us, and one that requires that we impose our will on everything that takes place. Slowly but surely we have everyone who works with us whipped into frenzied activity. There is little concern for the health or families of our colleagues. Discontent and grumbling begin and loyalty is seriously eroded. This pattern can be nothing but self-destructive. It is sometimes found in the old hierarchical, top-down model of leadership, but we can also find it in our communities and in our families. It leads to burnout, devaluation of the people who surround us, and the development of a manipulative style that isn't very effective in the long term. In fact, this style usually leads to situations of conflict, low productivity, and even derailment in a place of employment. This frenetic lifestyle can be compared to my experience on the lake. The person in this lifestyle is always canoeing in a storm without a compass. The determination of an ultimate destination is completely lost and we find ourselves paddling desperately just to stay afloat. Indeed, something is missing.

Sharon (not her real name) is a sad example of this style of self-destructive behavior. Sharon was appointed the CEO of an organization with more than three hundred employees when she was in her early forties. She was bright, articulate, caring, and creative, and had shown great promise as she moved up the ranks in the organization. Sharon's external behavior appeared to reflect strong values and inner strength. She was considered a balanced, well-grounded individual who valued the talents and gifts of the people with whom she worked. Everyone was extremely pleased at her appointment and anticipated an exciting future for the organization.

Sharon was determined to be a successful CEO, so determined that she buried herself in her work. Weekends, evenings, holidays all melted into one agenda for her—work. She was totally focused on becoming the company shining star. She began to ignore the talents of the people who surrounded her and to assume an authoritarian style of leadership. She insisted on making all final decisions, even in areas where there were individuals who were far more knowledgeable than she was. The impression she gave was that no one could do the job as perfectly as she could. Sharon had a drive for perfection that had not been recognized in her previous positions in the organization. She forgot the value of teamwork, of listening to the ideas of others, of delegating authority and responsibility, and of encouraging her employees to perform at peak efficiency. She forgot the generative power of introspection. She appeared to have lost all touch with the values that had gained her such respect. One by one, her loyal supporters began to question the wisdom of her appointment. They became disgruntled; they looked for every opportunity to criticize her work and blame her for mistakes that occurred. Outstanding employees left the company and a spirit of grumbling and dissatisfaction pervaded the organization.

Over time, the long hours and frequent conflict situations began to take their toll on Sharon's health. She became physically and mentally exhausted. She had completely lost sight of the needle on her internal compass. There was no balance in her life; she had immersed herself in a frenzy of activity. She had neither cultivated nor maintained her inner strength, her spirituality, her values. Sharon forgot that effective leadership is doing good things with the help of others. She thought that only she could make every right decision for the organization. She refused to listen to close friends who tried to help her recognize what was happening. Sadly, Sharon was eventually fired and never clearly understood what had happened. Sharon is an example of a person who lost sight of the need to develop her inner strength as well as her external skills. She saw her life in only one dimension, and that dimension was action.

At the other end of the spectrum, some individuals may be tempted to acquire a behavior that can be labeled *escapism*. In an awkward attempt to achieve some inner stability, these individuals may decide to carefully measure all activity and involvement so that they are not distracted from their lives of the spirit. They then live humdrum lives in which they avoid leadership at all costs. They involve themselves in decision making and activity only as it is required to maintain a decent living and a certain quality of life. To some extent, they become the passive sheep we talked about in the previous chapter. Of course, I hasten to add that I recognize that focusing primarily on spirituality can also become a form of action. For example, Thomas Merton, who spent most of his life in a Trappist monastery in Kentucky, saw and wrote about racism in the fifties with more insight than many of the activists of that period. Mother Teresa's work with the poor in India is known all over the world. Religious communities have long been recognized for their impact on issues of education and social justice. But we aren't discussing the benefits of choices of vocation in this chapter. We're talking about ordinary citizens and a style of leadership that is well balanced, one that operates with the spiritual values of peace, truth, right action, well-being, and love in places of employment, communities, and families.

It isn't necessary to choose between action and spirituality. We can and should develop both these dimensions of ourselves in our efforts to become good citizens and leaders. Our spirituality, our centeredness, is a vital and strong support for the many difficulties encountered in the active function of leadership. In a world where change is so rapid that what we have learned today may be inaccurate tomorrow, a balance of spirit, action, and faith in those around us is essential.

In truth, most of us allow ourselves to slip into an either-or mindset. We are clumsy in the process of achieving balance. First we immerse ourselves in the frenetic activity that we are led to believe will determine our success. Then we become totally exhausted and begin to function poorly, so we take a vacation! Sometimes we actually come back refreshed but promptly begin our frenetic round all over again, recognizing that we will soon need to plan for another vacation. At other times, we return to our jobs with regret—still tired—counting the months to our next vacation or the number of years to our retirement. What a depressing cycle! We tell ourselves that there has to be a better way—and there is. Simply stated, it is achieving a balanced approach to work and life by cultivating our spirituality. William C. Miller, cofounder and principal consultant for California-based Global Creativity Corporation, tells us, "How we put our spiritual values to work can make a huge difference to our own quality of life, and that also is the foundation for each organization in our society to become prosperous, successful, and healthy." [10] In other words, achieving a balanced life of spirituality and action can improve your own quality of life while making your contributions to an organization or your family more successful.

Core Values

Whether we choose an either-or existence or a balanced life is really a reflection of what we value. Stephen Covey, in *Principle-Centered Leadership,* tells us that "a compass has a true north that is *objective and external,* that reflects natural laws or *principles,* as opposed to values that are subjective and internal. Because the compass represents the verities of life, we must develop our value system with deep respect for 'true north' principles."[11] I believe values are critical to the growth and transformation of both people and organizations and that values are indicators of our spirituality. Values are priorities by which we choose to live our lives. They are designated in what we say, experienced through our feelings and imagination, and acted on repeatedly and consistently in our homes and places of work. Values, then, reflect our inner strength, our spirituality. As has been so well stated by Covey, our values should be established on principles that are proven, enduring guidelines for human behavior.[12] It is helpful to understand clearly this distinction between values and principles.

Whenever we begin a discussion that revolves around values, the question of whose values inevitably arises. Did the person who shot and killed the doctor who worked at the abortion clinic in Florida act on a set of values? Of course he did, but his values violated basic principles of human behavior. According to Covey, there exists in mankind "a universal belief in fairness, kindness, dignity, charity, integrity, honesty, quality, service and patience."[13] These are basic principles! Other authors speak about these basic principles as *core values*. As Miller says, "We may use different words, but the core values are always there: *inner peace, truth, right-conduct, nonviolence (which I like to call 'well-being'),* and, above all, *love.*"[14] What Miller addresses as core values is the same concept Covey outlines as basic principles. To avoid confusion, we need to develop a clear understanding of these terms.

Integration Is the Key

The story of John Howard Griffin provides a tangible example of the integration of action, core values, and spirituality. John is a white man who darkened his skin with chemicals to travel and experience the life of a black man in the South. He did this during the mid-fifties when the civil rights movement was gaining momentum, a time of great racial strife. Choosing to become a black man at this time placed him in a very risky position. John did this because he was determined to write a book that would expose the illusion of equality that was prevalent at that time in the United States, and allow him to experience the reality of racism.[15] His external behavior was a strong reflection of his inner strength, his spirituality. By his actions and his book, he made us much more aware of the reality of the times, and in turn he personally experienced a growth of inner strength.

We don't have to go all the way back to the fifties to find examples of individuals who have learned to depend on a balance of action and spirituality to get things done. In preparing to write this book, I have discovered many rich resources. Although it is sometimes difficult for individuals to express their faith and belief in the necessity of a deep spirituality to be a successful leader, I found a few who have been very articulate.

In 1975, while a freshman at Anderson College in Indiana, Rick Little (now president of the International Youth Foundation in Battle Creek, Michigan) was involved in a serious accident that completely changed his life. Driving back to the college from a weekend at home on a sleet-streaked January morning, he fell asleep at the wheel of his car. When he awoke, he found that he had broken his back. He spent the next six months in traction. This gave him six months to think, six months to reflect on his dysfunctional family life and his unsatisfactory educational experiences. His reflections led him to the conclusion that nothing in his education had prepared him for the alcoholism and suicidal tendencies of his mother, his father's inability to cope with the situation, and his own unexpected immobility.

Rick knew that his parents loved him deeply and that they had achieved a comfortable status in life with great effort and struggle. He also learned that their determination to work on controlling external forces with little emphasis on the spiritual had not been successful for them. He concluded that sheer will, intelligence, and determination can work on the external forces for a while, but one must achieve inner peace to maintain a stable environment. He was afraid that he would repeat the pattern of instability he was experiencing in his family. After Rick recovered from his injuries, he became involved with a Campus Life organization at Anderson College, where he found a mentor who asked him the key questions that led to his understanding of the importance of a spiritual role in achieving leadership and a well-balanced life.

The six months of Rick Little's confinement, the time he had to reflect on home and school experiences, turned out to be the beginning of his quest and his self-discovery. He was determined to find out if there were others who felt as poorly prepared to cope with the stresses of life as he was. As soon as his health allowed, he interviewed more than two thousand students in wealthy suburban schools and in poor inner-city schools. He discovered that, indeed, many of them were ill prepared to cope with the many demands of life that they would be forced to face. There was something missing. This led him to design a plan for a new kind of course for high school kids, a course designed around their concerns. The course would address responsibility, respect for self and others, reality and relationship skills, and the importance of developing inner strength. This was the beginning of *Quest,* five unique educational programs that have affected the lives of over four million youngsters ages five to eighteen in twelve thousand schools in twenty-nine countries and four continents.

For thirteen years, Rick worked to create this dynamic, new, and continually expanding program in school systems throughout the world. He began in a storefront with a refrigerator crate for a desk. Today the program operates from a thriving headquarters in Granville, Ohio, with a staff of 130 people. Rick is a man of tenacity, enthusiasm, energy, and belief in the importance of inner strength. These characteristics, in addition to his leadership ability, his recognition of the talents of his employees, and his ability to deal with the external environment, have helped him to maintain a sense of balance as he convinced corporations and foundations to support his efforts.

In January 1988, Rick Little started another organization, the International Youth Foundation. This organization is designed to identify the crisis issues for youth in many countries, to identify the most creative sources of power and authority in the country, and to bring them together to address the issues. Once again, Rick is leading by integrating action, core values, and spirituality around an issue that he has discovered is his passion.

Many people have achieved what may be evaluated as the external measures of success; yet like Rick they unexpectedly stumble upon an emptiness, a sense that something is missing. They suddenly feel the pain of isolation. They are missing the deep experience of balance with the underlying spiritual reality of life. We cannot rely on one dimension alone to experience the depth and breadth of life. "Humanity has always found inspiration in the simple, singular message of the spiritual traditions of the world: *All life is sacred and shares a common essence.* We are awakening to a need for leadership that speaks of this unity, a spiritual leadership that acts with a reverence for all life, in harmony with universal principles."[16]

Part Two

Pathways to Effective Leadership

There are many approaches to teaching leadership. Some scholars insist that one cannot teach the practical applications of leadership until the theory of leadership is understood. For them, the teaching of *theory* is prerequisite to the teaching of effective leadership action. Another perspective places emphasis on the *practice* of leadership and insists on an in-depth analysis of behavioral skills. Both approaches are legitimate, but for our purposes I have chosen to weave the theoretical and the practical aspects of leadership into a sometimes complex—but doable—art.

As I said in the Preface, you will find no earthshaking, amazing new discoveries about leadership in these pages. However, my goal is to transform the wealth of leadership knowledge into a form relevant for those of you who are not typically addressed in the business and political leadership literature. I hope that the chapters in this section—and the regular people you will meet along the way— will introduce you to a practical set of tools and resources to help you function more effectively as a compassionate and caring leader.

By using the weaving metaphor in Chapter Five, we will explore the power of building the capacity of people through inclusiveness. The chapter presents examples of the benefits and the difficulties of weaving a shared vision, as well as some tips and how-tos.

Chapter Six asks you to recognize the challenge of leading in a world that is growing increasingly smaller and more diverse. We will address the complexity of viewing situations through the many lenses of the multiple cultures now represented in our towns and cities. Only by learning that differences are neither right nor wrong, but merely different, can we open our minds to all points of view!

In Chapter Seven, you will gain some insight into the need for good communication and listening skills, as well as enjoy the humor of real stories about good and poor communication. Communication is a skill that affects people of all generations and walks of life.

Chapters Eight, Nine, and Ten, with the help of many examples, explore the styles and ethics of decision making, the willingness to take calculated risks, and the need to balance power and compassion. Chapter Eleven will help you understand resistance to change and the need for the leader to create an agenda for change. Whether we like change or not, it is inevitable! Chapter Twelve will remind you that having fun and managing stress are two important ingredients to successful leadership and followership. All work and no play can make Jack and Jill very dull people!

Chapter Thirteen addresses the need to take action where your talents are most needed. The Resources section at the end will give you some help and direction for further training, reading, and audiovisual media. The suggestions you will find on these pages barely dent the massive stocks of resources that are available. If those I have recommended are not sufficient, ask a librarian for more information.

There is much to be learned if we wish to function as twenty-first-century leaders. Although it would be impossible to include in one book all the information now available about leadership, the information in this section should provide you with a fuller understanding of the knowledge and skills needed to function as effective citizen leaders and followers. Practical suggestions from people who have succeeded—or failed, which can be even more useful—have also been included. Have fun with the short exercises. They will help you gain a better insight into what you know and what you still need to learn.

Chapter Five

Weaving a Shared Vision

Vision is not analytic; it is intuitive. It is knowing "in your bones" what can or must be done. In other words, vision isn't forecasting the future, it is creating the future by taking action in the present.
—James C. Collins and Jerry I. Porras

We've spent the past few chapters talking about the importance of finding your voice, of getting to know yourself and your passion. Now it's time to begin working on the skills necessary to reach your goals and become an effective leader. The skill of being able to create a vision is at the very heart of leadership. Yet most people confronted with the "vision thing" struggle for an understanding of it that is real and tangible. Because it doesn't seem to be something we can put our hands on, something we can touch, feel, and change, it seems difficult to understand. Some of the first questions that come to mind may well be: "How do I do it? What is it? How do I know when I have it? What actions do I take to discover it? How will others know about it?"

Personal Versus Shared Visioning

When you were a kid, did your imagination lead you to dream about the remarkable things you would do when you grew up? When you were a teenager, did you dream of traveling to far-away places and changing the world? When you got your first job, did you dream of being in a leadership role and changing the way things were done?

If so, you already have a good understanding of what a vision is. You may have even had some practical experience forming one. You may also recall that some of these dreams, which I will now call visions, were powerful motivational forces that affected your behavior. They propelled you into making choices that you thought might help you achieve that vision.

These can probably all be categorized as personal visions, but the same idea holds true in your role as a leader or follower in an organization or community. For example, let's suppose that you work as the manager of the telecommunications division for the LorCon International Communication Corporation. The vision of the company's founders is that LorCon International will be one of the most creative companies in the business, able to deliver services to educational institutions on time and at reasonable cost. They have built their company's vision around the needs of educational institutions. Your acceptance of the position of leader of the telecommunications area in this company indicates that you share that vision, that you will do everything possible to motivate your staff to share it as well, and you will do what it takes to contribute to achieving the dream. In this case, you were not the designer of the original vision, but you share it and have chosen to be a vital player in making the vision a reality. Obviously, you will also be achieving your personal vision of becoming an outstanding telecommunications team leader. Both these goals can only be accomplished when all the members of a team share in the desire to achieve the vision. We might call this a *shared vision*.

This concept of a shared vision also holds true in viewing a bigger picture beyond a place of employment; for example, in your role as a citizen of the United States. In this role you are part of the national vision. You share the responsibility as a citizen for the process of developing policies and carrying out the vision of the founding fathers of our country. The Constitution of the United States is a written description of the vision of the founding fathers. It sets some very clear democratic directions and values, but doesn't specify how to accomplish them. It does indicate that achieving these goals, this vision, requires the participation of all citizens. How do we participate? By voting, by serving in an elected office, or by contributing ideas at public forums. This was the original vision for a democratic society, and we as citizens of the United States have chosen to share that vision. We play an important part in making the

United States a better place to live and work. We can't delegate all that responsibility to our elected officials. It is impossible for them to accomplish such lofty goals alone. By choosing to become or remain citizens of the United States, we have chosen to share the vision of a democracy.

"What Is" and "What Could Be"

Simply stated, vision is first a dream and then a set of intentions. It is not mystical or religious. It is a sense of understanding intuitively what needs to be done, or a better way of accomplishing something. It is knowing "in your bones" an outcome, a goal, or direction and being able to communicate that sense of direction with enthusiasm and meaning. It is being able to maintain a dynamic tension between "what is" and "what could be."

Focusing completely on either one of these possibilities can lead to serious problems. If we spend our time ignoring everyday problems and obstacles while dreaming about "what could be," we have stepped out of the world of reality and turned into daydreamers. On the other hand, I am frequently struck by how quickly one can become totally absorbed in everyday nitty-gritty details, problems, and obstacles and forget the exciting possibilities the world offers. We all spend a lot of time dealing with "what is." We either like the way things are going and resist change, or we complain about the inefficiencies of the present situation. We complain about the traffic, the long wait for luggage at the airport, the cold food at the restaurant, or the poor communication at our workplace. How much time do we spend thinking about "what could be" and then forming a plan to make it happen? For most of us, the answer is "not much."

We've all heard the phrase, "If you don't know where you're going, it doesn't matter where you end up!" It is an extraordinary challenge to keep one eye on the reality of everyday problems and the other on exciting new possibilities. It is an even greater challenge to hear the visionary ideas of other members of a team and to incorporate them into a shared vision. A leader is a juggler, a person who maintains a dynamic vision of "what could be" while dealing with the everyday "what is" crises and mundane demands.

The following story shows us the power of dealing with both the "what is" and the "what could be." It is also an example of how one man, Jim Hathaway, persuaded an entire community to share his vision and enthusiasm. Jim Hathaway is the airport fire chief in Sioux City, Iowa. He formerly held the position of captain on the Sioux City fire department team and was the volunteer fire chief for the Air National Guard. The Sioux City airport is small and had never had a team of firefighters exclusively for its safety. The city leaders assumed that the city fire department could handle any fire that might occur at their little airport. Jim, his National Guard commander, and others were not comfortable with this situation. Jim began a process of convincing the city leaders of the need for a fire-fighting team exclusively for the airport. This idea met with much resistance. Many residents of the community believed it to be a superfluous add-on, costing unnecessary tax dollars. They didn't share his vision. However, in 1987, the city managers—persuaded by Jim and his commanding officer—made the decision to have a fire-fighting team exclusively for the airport. This was a very controversial decision, but would affect many lives in just two short years.

Jim was appointed chief of the new team. He immediately took action. In addition to hiring and organizing a staff, he also undertook the rewriting of a disaster plan. This, too, was viewed by many with skepticism and criticism. Jim convinced the skeptics that "every city should expect some kind of disaster." He was a visionary and a planner and he believed his team and the city should be prepared for *anything* that might happen. His team shared his vision and they worked together to consolidate a mutually agreed-upon plan.

Jim and his team put together some very robust, very realistic, full-day exercises to practice the disaster response. He also worked hard to make certain that all the local agencies, fire departments, hospitals, city and county police forces, emergency reaction teams, airport traffic controllers, and Air National Guard leaders shared in the development of this plan and worked cooperatively to ensure a prompt and effective response to any pending disaster. He put a great deal of effort into weaving this as a shared vision of excellence and teamwork. It took many hours of hard work; it didn't happen overnight! When asked why he did this in a place like Sioux City, Jim said, "I think that I had a vision, a burning desire to accomplish this. I didn't know why, but I knew there was a reason and we should be prepared."

His intuition proved to be correct and his vision of excellence in planning, collaboration, and response to a disaster were indeed challenged. Most of us can recall the July 1989 crash of a DC-10 in a Sioux City cornfield. Flight 232, loaded with 296 passengers, was en route from Denver to Chicago when it crashed outside Sioux City. Despite the tremendous impact, fire, heat, and chaos, 180 people survived. They survived because the disaster team of Sioux City was well prepared to respond to any emergency. Jim Hathaway—his intuition, his planning, his vision of excellence, and his ability to convince people of the value of working together—was the one most responsible for this extraordinary feat. Jim will tell you that it was the leadership of each of the many teams that deserves the credit. In one sense he is correct; but someone had to take the lead in *weaving the shared vision*—and that person was Jim.

Jim, as leader of the airport fire team, had a vision of "what could be." He also had the organizational and planning skills to mobilize a group of people to design an orderly process to achieve that vision. In any case, when creating and weaving a shared vision, you must also have a plan to achieve that vision.

In Sioux City, the vision was one of excellent performance in response to a disaster. Jim's plan and skill in persuading the team to practice and work together, sometimes more than nine hours a day for each exercise, proved more than satisfactory when the disaster actually occurred. The key to this accomplishment was Jim's ability to connect with people in a meaningful way and to persuade them to change their ideas about what was or was not necessary. This could not be accomplished through giving orders, coercion, or manipulation. People must be persuaded to freely and enthusiastically make their own unique contributions to shaping the vision as theirs, must acknowledge their essential role in accomplishing it, and then, and then only, will they participate fully with energy and excitement.

As tragic as the airline accident was, the outcome served to convince the community of the value of working together. Saving 180 lives certainly confirmed the effectiveness of the new collaborative ways adopted by the Sioux City community. Jim and his team members now spend time teaching other communities the value of sharing a vision and working together.

Warren Bennis and Burt Nanus, long-time scholars of leadership, say, "Only a few will lead nations, but more will lead companies. Many more will lead departments or small groups. Those who aren't department heads will be supervisors. Those who follow on the assembly line may lead at the union hall."[1] In all these situations, as well as many more, the process of weaving a shared vision is of primary importance.

Four Visioning Skills

As you strive to understand what it means to be an effective *visionary* leader, there are four skills you need to refine:

- *The skill to allow yourself to dream,* to open your mind to new possibilities, to cultivate your intuition and to be willing to develop a coherent, compelling vision.
- *The skill to involve everyone who might be affected* by the vision so that they all know and feel they are a part of the endeavor. The vision then becomes a shared vision and people are empowered to pursue the goal.
- *The skill to understand that the process of leading is seamlessly bound to the process of following.* In achieving the vision you may find yourself performing in both these capacities.
- *The skill to jointly establish a framework or a plan of action, to achieve the vision.*

Creating the Vision

Visioning is an art and skill you can use on a daily basis. The art is to be able to design a futuristic portrait of yourself or of your environment using facts, fantasies, fiction, and fun. The part that is skill is the act of training yourself to think about tomorrow and beyond with no inhibitions and to design plans for how to get there.

In the previous chapter, we discussed the value of maintaining a balanced lifestyle, allowing yourself time for action and time to relax, to think, to develop inner strength, and to enjoy the people and things around you. This ability is very important to the process of visioning. People have different ways of accomplishing this goal. Some people find time for visioning in a quiet evening alone, or listening to classical or mood music, or while driving to work, waiting for a bus, or even sitting at the airport. Some devote a few minutes to the effort before they fall asleep. I find long walks in the woods or a park where I can admire the beauties of nature very invigorating and helpful to the process of futuristic thinking.

Once you have established the place or the time that you find most relaxing, then begin practicing the art and the skill of creating your vision. Remember, the skill is training yourself to plan not only for tomorrow, but for years into the future. The art is opening your mind and your heart to your intuition and your dreams. You can either practice creating a vision for yourself personally or you can practice weaving a shared vision for yourself within an organization or community. Let's practice a little right now!

First, clear your mind of all the nitty-gritty problems of your day. Tune in to your favorite relaxing situation or environment. Then begin to create a vision of the future. Allow yourself to travel forward in time, as far as you can, even all the way to retirement, and stay open to all your hopes and dreams. Of course, the practical part of your brain will interfere with this activity by telling you that this is foolish, that you'll be embarrassed, that this is just a waste of time. Try to suppress these feelings during this reflective time and dream of yourself in ten, twenty, even thirty years. Dare to see yourself in ways and places you truly would like to be. Ask yourself the questions in Exhibit 5.1.

These questions are just the first step toward establishing your own personal vision. This first step is also necessary in establishing a shared organizational, family, or community vision. Obviously some additional skills such as listening, communication, building trust, and a sense of humor are needed to weave a shared vision that includes the ideas and dreams for a community or organization. We'll talk more about these relational skills in subsequent chapters.

Many excellent organizations have well-developed training programs designed to move groups of people toward a shared vision of the future. The Disney University is one such organization. You can find others listed in Resource A. Walt Disney was a very creative man. He is credited with the statement, "If you can dream it, you can do it."[2] You may want to pause in your reading now and allow yourself to do a little more dreaming.

Weaving a Shared Vision

I have used the phrase "weaving a shared vision" several times now. I like the metaphor of weaving because it presents a visual image of the process of uniting the dreams of all the people involved in any

Exhibit 5.1. Creating Your Own Vision.

What is your environment like as you look around you?

_____

What role are you playing in this new environment?

_____

Who else is a part of your vision?

_____

Are you proud of the way in which you see yourself?

_____

Are you living up to your full potential?

_____

Are others pleased to be associated with you?

_____

What have you accomplished?

_____

Have you made a difference?

_____

What is still to be accomplished?

_____

project. The dreams or visions of each person can be considered as single threads in the weaving of the overall design of the fabric of the vision. Each person brings a different talent, strength, spirit, and fire to developing and accomplishing the vision. After creating a personal vision and establishing some plans to achieve it, it is important to discover whether your vision is achievable within the organization or community where you find yourself. If you conclude that it is, then the next important action is to communicate your vision and listen to the dreams of others. This is an important step before attempting to weave a shared vision that addresses a common good. *This vision will be a powerful force for change only if all the individuals involved in the organization enthusiastically believe in the vision and see their own personal goals and dreams integrally woven into the fabric of the plan.*

As we bring the threads together in weaving the fabric of the vision, we find that the strength and beauty that evolve are far greater as a whole fabric than they were as individual threads or ideas. Likewise, as we weave this shared vision for our community or organization, we will discover that the individuals involved will exhibit enthusiasm, loyalty, hard work, and love if they believe that they have contributed a valuable and respected part of the vision. Their commitment and dedication will be evident in everything they do.

The accomplishments of a young Native American woman in Wisconsin clearly reflect the value of this process of weaving a shared vision. Deborah Doxtator, at twenty-eight years of age, was elected vice chairperson of the 10,200-strong Oneida Nation of Wisconsin. Now at age thirty she is the tribal chairwoman. That's quite an accomplishment for such a young woman! Deborah's dream, her vision, had been to become a leader of her tribe. Now she had achieved her personal vision and her next challenge was to listen and weave a shared tribal vision. Deborah's primary challenge in this role was to serve in a leadership capacity during a demanding time of transition. Her tribe was moving from a period of constant deficit to one of very rapid financial growth due to the initiation of legalized gambling. Moving from poverty to wealth wisely is a tough task for anyone. For an entire tribe, it was a tremendous challenge.

To accomplish this transition successfully, it was evident to Deborah that she had to listen to the hopes and dreams of each and every individual involved. She had to pull all these dreams together into a shared vision. According to Deborah, everyone had an idea about what their special needs were; this was the expression of their individual visions. They had been living with very limited resources; now they were too quickly faced with abundant resources and they had no shared vision or *common goal* for the effective use of these new funds. She said, "It seemed that we were constantly running into problems with people who had not done enough thinking, dreaming, or planning. People would submit large budgets every year, but they didn't have a plan to go along with it." Deborah recognized that the tribal leaders had not taken the time to reflect upon or develop a vision of the future for the community. Nor did they have any concept of how each individual agency or unit contributed to the big picture of the future of the tribe. Because of Deborah's earlier position as grants writer for the tribe, she had a much better "big picture" of the needs and desires of the various organizations and units. It was up to Deborah to weave the hopes and dreams of each individual and each tribal organization into a tapestry of the future for the tribe.

Deborah's first task was to convince the tribal leadership and committee members that her vision included all of them, and that it would incorporate the culture and integrity of the tribe and its customs. Her task was to firmly, but gently, move her people from the "what is" to the "what could be"—from individual visions to a shared vision that addressed the common good.

Some people like change and feel motivated and challenged by it. They see change as a sign of hope or deliverance from the status quo. Change to them is a sign of life and a brighter future. They are usually inspired by the opportunity to shape the future and find courage in dreaming about "what could be." Other people seem to respond to any and all change as a disturbance of their comfort zone. They are annoyed by the very suggestion of change and when it is inevitable, they are filled with anxiety or depression. Deborah found herself dealing with all these emotions as she worked with her people. She faced many very difficult and even life-threatening situations while trying to listen and persuade as required to weave a tribal vision.

Under Deborah's leadership, retreats and training sessions were held to bring together the members of the committees and subcommittees that formed the leadership of the tribe. Through these experiences, the people were able to get to know and understand each other. Gradually, conflicts were resolved and an atmosphere of trust and listening was cultivated. People who feared change and had no conception of an overall vision for the tribe began to understand where their individual contributions would fit and be respected. This process was difficult and took a great deal of time and patience. Modern planning, development, and visioning techniques were used, and the culture and traditions of the Oneida tribe were carefully protected. Although time-consuming and sometimes painful, out of these exercises grew the "Seventh Generation Planning Process."

The success of the tribe can be attributed to Deborah's insight into the complex, time-demanding process of developing a shared vision. By weaving the concerns and needs of the entire organization into the goals of the top governmental body of the tribe, everyone assumed both the responsibility and the rewards for the success of the enterprise. Deborah enthusiastically says, "Leadership is in valuing people and each person valuing the other. That is the best way we can provide leadership in our communities—by valuing each other. Recognizing the skills and talents each of us brings to the table creates community."

Effective leadership can create an environment that encourages dialogue and sharing. This is accomplished by communicating a vision with enthusiasm, spirit, excitement, and conviction but in such a way that others feel they can add to it, take away from it, and share in its development. Belonging to a group, especially a group that is making a difference, can be a very powerful motivating factor. When people know that they have helped to develop and are working for something bigger than themselves, they can be expected to be loyal, dependable, and inspired. An environment is created that fosters the idea that at some point in achieving the goals, everyone will be expected to lead when their talents are needed and to energetically follow when others take the lead. Rather than top-down, forced direction, it becomes a coherent, collaborative framework that has been refined and enriched by each person's contribution.

Only when all the individuals involved enthusiastically accept their role as part of the vision does it acquire the force necessary to change an organization or community and move it in the intended direction. Fundamentally, this is what leadership at its best is all about—it moves us to touch higher places within ourselves and others, and it enables us to communicate a sense of inspiration, unity, and energy to members of our group. It takes courage and toughness to create and hold to a shared vision and to connect with people in a meaningful way, so that they see their personal visions as one with the vision for the organization. It takes even more courage to persevere when reality does not immediately reward our efforts. The actions of both Deborah and Jim reflect this courage and perseverance.

Don't forget that intuition is frequently an important part of creating a vision. As with Jim Hathaway, that gut feeling that something must be done is intuition. Consequently, vision often has the appearance of being opposed to the rational. This may not be a major problem when things are going as you had hoped, but when things are not going so well, when the vision is being condemned as irrational, to hold tight to a vision and to encourage those who have shared this vision with you takes will, toughness, and intention! Some may even interpret this as stubbornness, but if you have listened carefully to the views of others, then trust your intuition and find ways to move toward your goal.

The process of creating a shared vision is something that can be learned by anyone and taught to everyone. It should be denied to no one. Bennis and Nanus stress that leaders gain the attention of those around them by creating a vision that develops from an unparalleled concern about the outcome of some specific situation.[3] I would add that these leaders, like Jim and Deborah, also have the skill to weave the hopes and dreams of all the players into an outcome that serves everyone.

A shared vision evolves when we first allow ourselves to dream, then get in touch with the hopes and dreams of the people involved, and lastly communicate a sense of purpose. A leader who understands weaving a shared vision listens carefully to the loud proclamations, the quiet whisperings, and even to what is not being said! Yes, anyone can learn the process of developing a shared vision, but not everyone has the courage and patience to put the process into practice.

Leading and Following to Achieve the Vision

When change is rapid, no single individual can expect to serve as leader all the time and in every situation. All of us should strive to learn to be leaders and followers who are willing to assume the responsibility to weave a shared vision, establish a framework to accomplish the vision, and then *act as the servants of this vision*. In the course of a single day, each of us may find ourselves involved in all these processes—dreaming, planning, and implementing. It appears to me that the future will continue to demand the interdependence of independent people in the workplace and in their communities. People are eager to participate. They want to play an important role in achieving a vision that they helped to create. The authoritarian model of leadership will no longer be acceptable or feasible.

Effective leadership and strong, supportive followership skills are critical to the success of any endeavor. Do you know your strengths and limitations? Are you practicing your visioning skills? Are you willing to empower others to achieve a common vision? Are you a strong, supportive follower when the leadership of someone else is needed? Take some time to reflect on these questions. What steps can you take to strengthen your capacity in these areas?

Whether working with an organization, a community group, or your own family, it is important to recognize that clarity and power of vision can come from the creative output of any individual. Recognizing this, it becomes your responsibility to acknowledge your strengths and limitations, and then ensure that every person has recognized and accepted his or her own personal potential within the framework of the values and good of the whole. With this new way of thinking and acting, *leadership and followership then make their claims on everyone.* Common sense tells us that "not everyone can or should contribute in the same way. Nor will everyone participate all the time."[4] What each individual does and when depends on that individual's abilities and willingness to recognize when those talents are needed. The next step is to take the initiative and to respond positively to others' initiatives.[5]

You will discover that the sharing of the responsibility as a leader or as a follower for the accomplishment of a shared vision injects dignity and commitment into the relationships. This, indeed, may be the major role of leaders of the future, to empower others to lead and to make self-worth, dignity, and commitment possible in others. This new way of thinking can serve as a powerful tool to foster leadership throughout our society and at all levels of our organizations.

From Vision to Action

A vision is little more than an empty pipe dream until it is widely shared and accepted. We all know people who have extraordinary dreams, but never seem to be able to get beyond the dream stage. They are unwilling or unable to exert the effort necessary to share the dream and weave the creative ideas of others into the plan for accomplishing the vision. It is not enough to have a vision; you must have a sufficient level of courage, intention, and openness to other ideas to carry out the vision. Anyone can create a vision—with a little practice—but it takes a leader with guts and drive to move it out into the world of reality. Burt Nanus makes the point much more clearly than I can, saying, "By this point, it should be obvious that there is no single thing you can do to 'make it happen'—that is, to ensure that your vision is successfully implemented. Communication alone won't do it, no matter how eloquent and persuasive you are. Organizational changes alone won't do it, no matter how appropriate they may be or how great an impact they have on the organization. Effective individual participation or teamwork alone won't do it either, no matter how competent or well supported."[6] Only when all these factors are appropriately in place, and a shared plan of action has been agreed upon, can we successfully move from a daydream to a reality.

In most discussions on leadership, talking about a plan of action is the point where people begin to question and challenge the likenesses and differences between leadership and management. From my perspective, the two are an essential partnership. The process of weaving a shared vision is in danger of falling apart unless a degree of order and consistency, a plan of action, is in place. This plan is the essential piece needed to move the group from the dream to the reality.

In my many leadership roles throughout my own life and career, it has become very clear to me that I am energized by working with people to generate ideas and develop visions of "what could be." What has also become very clear to me is that I don't like and am not very good at deciding the intricate and multiple details needed to achieve the vision. I have learned that having the ideas and enthusiastically communicating them are not enough. Building a shared vision is not enough! I have discovered that the power to achieve a vision is multiplied many times over if I surround myself with people who have the strengths and skills that I lack. By weaving the substance of their strength into the fabric of the vision, I have discovered that we will evolve an orderly plan that will propel us toward our goal.

Simply stated, the visioning process sets the direction for useful change, and the strategic planning process develops an orderly process to achieve the vision. However, it is much more complex than that. All of us can point to leaders who had wonderful and visionary ideas, but who were very disruptive when asked to deal with an orderly planning process. Likewise, we can recall examples of people who were both visionary and able to produce a very orderly change process. We can also recall individuals who were so intensely involved in intricate details of the plan that they completely lost sight of where they were going! They were captured by the details.

Effective leadership is skilled at weaving a shared vision for change that will improve the lives of those involved. Effective leaders are also wise enough to know that good planning is needed to achieve the vision. Intricately bound to these visioning skills are the attributes of collaboration, communication, decision making, risk taking, commitment, love, compassion—and a sense of humor.

So, how do we capture the imagination of others and inspire them to move toward a vision? How do we communicate and weave the hopes and dreams of people into a shared vision? How do we develop an understanding of the kaleidoscope of differences and beauty in the ideas of others? Mastery of collaboration and understanding of the depth and breadth of the contributions of other cultures and people are invaluable to developing a shared vision. This mastery is a vital aspect of the essence of effective leadership in today's society. The following chapter will help you reach for greater depth and insight in understanding the rich contributions of diversity and individual differences in developing a shared vision.

Chapter Six

Appreciating a Kaleidoscope of Views

Individuals who collaborate see each situation from many different angles, generate creativity, and learn from one another.
—GIFFORD PINCHOT AND ELIZABETH PINCHOT

As we have seen, developing a shared vision is not an easy task. It is time consuming and complex! It takes courage, confidence, and the ability to recognize the value of different points of view. It would be a complex process even in an environment made up of individuals who appear to be culturally very much alike. Despite comparable skin color and ethnic heritage, we would quickly discover that not everyone learns, thinks, feels, senses, or is motivated to action in the same way. Indeed, with all else remaining the same, even the different points of view of men as compared to women in approaching and solving problems are something to be reckoned with in the process of weaving a shared vision.

However, take a look around you. Our world is rapidly becoming smaller and more interdependent. Our communities and organizations reflect a tremendous range of cultural differences and viewpoints. If we were to carefully analyze the food we eat, the cars we drive, and the tools we use, we would discover that they represent the endeavors of people found in the four corners of the earth! The demographics of the nineties and statistical projections for the year 2000 clearly point toward an increasingly diverse society. The

1987 Hudson Institute report, *Workforce 2000*, indicates that minorities and women will account for almost 80 percent of the growth of the labor force between now and the year 2000.[1] It also tells us that white males will account for only 15 percent of the new additions to the U.S. workforce.[2] It is hard to believe that the face of our workplaces and communities will be so different. Obviously these workforce projections are also indicators of the changing face of our communities. The demands of this new environment will challenge our creativity, our willingness to learn about and understand different cultures, and our openness to other points of view.

Whenever I talk about the changing face of our society, I like to use the example of a kaleidoscope. Most of us have had one of these fascinating toys during our lifetime. That little instrument uses items of various colors, shapes, sizes, and textures to create a vast array of very beautiful pictures. Not one of the individual particles inside the kaleidoscope loses its individuality or distinctive beauty, but they all lend themselves to the creation of a stream of fascinating visions that together are far more beautiful than each one would have been alone.

To create successful organizations and communities of the future, we need to learn the lesson of the kaleidoscope. We need to value the richness of diversity. We need to find ways to draw on the unique strengths of every member so as to effect change of lasting value to the quality of life.

Leaders can no longer succeed by viewing situations through the singular lens of their own specialization or culture. Better listening and collaborative skills are required for this new environment. Incorporating these skills into our thinking and allowing each individual the freedom of personal expression give us the opportunity to appreciate a whole situation.

Valuing Diversity

Our natural tendency is to gravitate toward people who look like us, speak like us, think like us, and live like us. We usually prefer to work with people who are educated in the same disciplines or at the same schools. Sometimes we even segregate ourselves by gender. Have you ever been at a party or meeting when all the men congregate on one side of the room and all the women on the other? Of course, we all have. Yet nothing can destroy a team or limit the collaborative process in communities and organizations faster than the unwillingness to listen and value other points of view. Nothing can kill creative potential more rapidly than this tendency toward sameness.

This struggle to remain the same goes on every day and is being experienced in many large and small communities all across the country. For example, let's look at the city of Santa Fe, New Mexico. It is a very old, lovely city. Many generations of Hispanics and Native Americans have made this charming place their home. Recently, it has become a mecca for wealthy people from all over the country. These individuals, primarily Anglos, are trying to recreate the all-alike communities and comfort levels they had in their places of origin. They appear to completely ignore and disrespect Santa Fe's long history of diversity, and have attempted to create a very insular environment for themselves. I use the word *appear* because their attitude may not have been deliberate. Nevertheless, this attitude has caused a great deal of tension in this old city, which has historically worked to maintain a true sense of community among its diverse cultures.

In 1994, the newly elected mayor of Santa Fe thought that a first step toward building and healing relationships, easing tensions, and reestablishing community might be to develop a day of celebration on the plaza. She called the plan Community Day. The people of the community were asked to volunteer their services to help make this a day to enjoy ethnic food, music, art, and crafts— and to get a better understanding of the diversity represented in Santa Fe and to help create a sense of connection.

Trying to put a planning group together for this event became a real struggle. People of each cultural heritage were suspicious and tended to associate only with people of the same cultural heritage. After several unsuccessful efforts, the exasperated mayor called upon Ron Zee and his team at Santa Fe Community College for help. Why Ron Zee? Because Ron, although he is an Anglo, has shown his awareness of the richness of cultural diversity. When Ron was hired at the college to direct a project on intercultural relationships, he immediately recognized the need to respond to the rich diversity of the community. He hired a staff that was broadly representative of the city of Santa Fe. Hispanics and Native Americans were the majority; he deliberately remained the only Anglo on the staff.

The mayor recognized the cultural sensitivity reflected in Ron's team and believed this was the perfect group to help make the Community Day happen. The team accepted the mayor's challenge and became the catalysts, the motivators, of the community celebration. They actively participated in the planning and in the event itself. The people of the many different cultural groups grew to trust them because they saw themselves represented on the organizing team. The people of the community worked hard to make it happen because they believed they were represented in all phases of the process of leading, planning, developing, and implementing the celebration. The kaleidoscope of views had come together, and the picture that evolved was inclusive and satisfying to everyone. The day was a great success.

The following year, Ron's team was not available to assist with the program development. However, he thought that working with the intercultural planning team (his staff) of the previous year had served as a learning experience for the community, demonstrating a successful, diverse model. He acknowledges with deep regret that the lesson was not well learned. The project again experienced difficulties. According to Ron, the newly organized planning team did not reflect the many cultures of Santa Fe; it was primarily Anglo. This group struggled to get the participation of all the ethnic groups in the community. They were met with resistance, suspicion, and disinterest. Ron said, "We told them from the very beginning, you need to pull together a planning group reflective of the community broadly. If you pull from only one segment of the community initially, it is going to be difficult to get others to participate."

The experience in Santa Fe certainly represents the natural tendency to gravitate toward people who are just like us, to seek ideas that might as well have been cloned from our own. However, this behavior can only lead to failed projects. Today in the United States, almost every community is experiencing rapid change and growth in the number of new and different cultures represented in the community. In this environment, developing the skills of relationship building should be first and foremost before any attempt is made to develop the skills of problem solving. According to Ron Zee, who has a deep love for his community, "As we become a more diverse society, we have to spend more time listening to each other, telling our stories and establishing relationships based on trust and understanding." These are wise words from a man who is living the experience.

Stephen Covey, the well-known human development author and instructor, says:

> Cloning produces negative energy, because it inhibits the full expression of a person's talents and gifts. On the other hand, building a complementary team—which has one goal but many different roles, perceptions, methods, and approaches—enables the full expression of talents and releases positive energy.
>
> Why is the tendency to clone so prevalent and so strong? Because cloning gives leaders a false sense of security. When you have people thinking like you, doing like you, speaking like you, referring to you, quoting you, dressing like you, and grooming like you, then you feel that you're being validated as a leader. You feel that you have value, because other people value being like you.[3]

Opening our hearts and heads to the new complexity of our communities and workplaces is a demanding process that needs to be nurtured. Leaders should assume the responsibility to build an understanding of diversity into the culture and core value system of an organization or community. It will take more than a one-time experience or training session, as Santa Fe discovered, and it will certainly not happen by itself. Perhaps most important, this building process should include everyone—all employees, all community members, women and men, all age groups, all levels of education, management and nonmanagement, all personalities, *all people*. Whatever process is used to achieve this goal, it should be a process that recognizes and values differences—gender differences, ethnic differences, and just plain differences in point of view! Then and then only will an environment be created in which everyone can work together with respect and dignity to weave a shared vision, and each person will be proud to achieve his or her highest potential.

Trends

Let's look at some of the long-term social trends that have been observed by various research groups around the country. Leaders will have to keep these trends in mind to be effective in an environment that is global and changing radically. These trends are changing the way we live, work, and do business and in so doing they are demanding a new kind of leadership, a leadership that values diversity and respects all individuals. In addition to the workplace changes mentioned earlier as projected by the Hudson Institute, we have the following to reckon with:

- *We have an aging society.* More elderly are living longer.
- *We also have a middle-aging society.* The baby boom generation is now putting a growing population bulge in the thirty-five to fifty-five age group.
- *The education level of the population is increasing.* The number of adults with some college will be close to 60 percent by 2000. This is up from 20 to 30 percent at the present time.
- *Attitudes toward authority are changing.* Confidence in the leadership of institutions (the presidency, the army, Congress, lawyers, churches, the press) began dropping sharply in the late 1960s and continues to decline. Meanwhile, intellectual property and finance are growing in importance. Financial transactions and trade *in ideas* will grow two to three times faster than the world gross domestic product.
- *Advances in information and communication technologies will continue* to speed up our lives and add challenges.
- *There will be expanding choices for people.* Products and educational opportunities once available only to a few are now readily available via technology.[4]

Add to these social trends the demographic changes taking place and we have a vivid kaleidoscope indeed! According to the 1989 U.S. Bureau of the Census projection for the next forty years, we can anticipate the following:

- The white population will increase by only 25 percent.
- The African American population will increase by 68 percent.
- The Asian American, Pacific Island American, and American Indian populations will increase by 79 percent.
- The Latino or Hispanic population will increase by 187 percent.[5]

This basic information is a wake-up call to all of us. We must be prepared to learn about and understand age differences, gender differences, background differences, color differences, educational differences, cultural differences, and technological differences. The learning environment in these changing communities will demand active listening and an openness to learning something new every single day.

Community

All these factors add to the many lenses through which the individuals in our communities and organizations perceive reality. To go about the process of developing the skill to build dynamic organizations that respect the interdependence of independent people of many different points of view, it is important, as we saw in Chapter Two, to have a clear understanding of yourself, that is:

- Who are you?
- What are your strengths and limitations?
- What is your passion?
- Have you found your voice?

Then we need to clarify our personal understanding of community, team building, and collaboration. What is your definition of community? Do you live in one? Work in one? Is community a neighborhood to you? A group of people interested in the same issue? Is it a way of thinking? Do we still have communities in the United States? Do you belong to a community? How do you know? Answers to these questions are more complex than you might think.

People argue about the definition of community all the time. Many focus the definition very narrowly and think of it as a neighborhood or place. Others insist that it is a group of people interested in the same field or issue regardless of place. For our purposes we will use the definition made popular by M. Scott Peck, an author of several books on the subject of community.

Peck has provided an excellent guide to community in his book, *The Different Drum*. His idea of community reflects what society and work life could be. To him, community is not a noun (a specific geographical spot) but rather it is a verb, a form of behavior. According to Peck, *"Community is a spirit."*[6] This spirit of community is inclusive. It doesn't exclude anyone who wants to be a part of it.[7] It encourages differences so that just like the kaleidoscope, the picture of the whole will have much more depth, beauty, and intensity than the individual.

The word *spirit* may be as intangible to you as the word vision! However, I'm sure you have felt it at some time in your life. This spirit of community is frequently experienced at a time of great crisis. When the terrorist bomb in Oklahoma caused the federal building to collapse and hundreds of men, women, and children were injured or killed, people from every walk of life worked together night and day to rescue the injured. Many of us, hundreds of miles away, opened our hearts and our wallets to people we had never met as we suddenly recognized our own vulnerability and common humanity. Men and women of every race and persuasion put their hearts and bodies into the effort of working for a common cause. This is the spirit we need to strive for if we hope to achieve the same results in times other than crisis. Once people experience the spirit of community, they have a feeling of nostalgia and a desire to achieve it again. It is intoxicating! This collective spirit, this interdependence of independent people, needs to be nurtured to make our workplaces and communities productive places in the next century.

I also like the metaphor used by community builder Kazimierz Gozdz: "It [community] is not like a stew in which all the ingredients are cooked so long that they are a gooey mass. Instead, community is like a crisp salad in which all the ingredients (in this case people) retain their individuality, yet make something greater than the sum of the parts.

"With true community, there has to be commitment, a willingness to coexist. It is not a leaderless group but rather a group of leaders. All capabilities in the group are utilized in a flow in which different people lead or contribute when it is appropriate."[8] The key words here are "lead or contribute when it is appropriate." This assumes that every member of the community is recognized and practices as a leader and a supportive follower. It reaffirms the interdependence of independent people.

If we take into account the trends I shared with you earlier, you will immediately recognize the need to incorporate this thinking into our acts of leadership and followership. We cannot and should not stop the flow of diverse people into our lives. They bring a richness that we should celebrate. Weaving the tapestry of the shared vision of a group that reflects the wisdom of age, the spontaneity of youth, the rich cultural differences of people of color, and the different points of view of women juxtaposed with those of men can be a breathtaking, positive experience.

Most of our communities or places of work are too large to operate as a "committee of the whole." We need to form smaller groups with specific responsibilities to achieve the common goal. You may recall from Chapter Five how Jim Hathaway in Sioux City, Iowa, had teams of firefighters, social workers, police, doctors, nurses, and city administrators all playing important parts to achieve a common goal of excellence in response to a disaster. These smaller groups may be composed of a great variety of independent people with comparable skills and training. They need to operate as a *team*. So how do we go about building teams of people that will then collaborate with each other? How do we keep in mind the good of the entire community or organization, while recognizing the interdependence of very independent individuals? Will finding the most talented people in the community or organization do it? Let's do some thinking about this process and look at some examples of successful and unsuccessful teams.

Team Building

Let's suppose that you agree that working together for a common purpose sounds exciting and productive. So you have carefully selected a talented, diverse group of people in your community or organization, shared the objectives for bringing them together and—*nothing happens!* In fact, not only is it impossible to get them to communicate their ideas and dreams to weave a shared vision, but there is actually an electrified air of tension every time this diverse group meets. *What have you done wrong?*

Probably nothing, but you cannot assume that by bringing talented people together you will automatically have a team.[9] You just have a group of talented people—who have no idea how to become a team. They need help in understanding how their unique contributions can be strengthened by recognizing and encouraging the unique talents of the other members of the group. They need to understand what is expected of them. They need education and training in the concepts of team building. They need to know what it takes to move from a dysfunctional group to a dynamic team.[10] Sports history is filled with examples of the failure of teams to perform successfully despite the effort to assemble as many superstars as possible. The chemistry wasn't right; the stars were unable to integrate their efforts toward the overall goal of team victory.

That same chemistry may be missing in your first attempts to bring people together in your community or workplace to work toward a common goal. This is not unusual. The process takes time, patience, dedication, and a leader with the skills to coach and facilitate the group. Team building means taking deliberate action to identify talent, discover and remove barriers, and help people change their behavior and replace it with the actions that can lead to successful leadership. Teamwork is the work of many—it cannot be accomplished by one person, no matter how talented that one person may be.

When people are brought together to form groups, each person brings a personal set of knowledge, skills, values, and vision. Only when each one comes to an understanding that the whole is greater than the sum of the parts will they function and be recognized as a *team*. Only when each member accepts credit for successes and equal responsibility for failures will the team be creative and dynamic. Psychologists and sociologists have long studied what might be called the stages of team building. Let's briefly discuss these stages.[11]

The first stage of team building is sometimes called the *Forming Stage*. So much interpersonal and individual investigation is going on at this point that little or nothing relevant to the purpose of organizing as a group may be accomplished. As a leader and facilitator you need to be patient; don't let all the preening and prancing worry you. Remember, *teams are made up of people*. The undercurrents during the Forming Stage will reflect very human reactions. There will be a concern for personal identity—people will wonder if they belong, if they will fit in, if they will have any influence on the group, and if they can trust the others who are potentially part of the team. There will be concerns about relationships within the group. And, as is normal with most groups, there will be a need to establish trust and openness.

If we persevere through this preliminary stage, then the group will move to the second stage of team building, sometimes identified as the *Storming Stage*. This is a very, very difficult stage to accept. Many groups never get beyond this stage and the entire experience becomes one of frustration and nonproductivity. It is extremely important to understand group process and conflict resolution so as to help the group work through this stage. Group process is basically people respectfully dealing with other people. Much of what we are talking about in this section of the book concerns group process. Effective leadership and team building cannot be accomplished without knowing yourself and understanding the processes of the interactions of people.

During this period of team building, it is important to allow the individuals involved to take the time to work out their relationships with the members of the group. Everybody seems to know the right way to achieve the vision. No one wants to listen or collaborate. People begin to choose sides, there is disunity, tension, jealousy, and finally disgust. Sometimes there is little energy left to progress toward the real goal. Usually, with good facilitation, which is the leader's role, individuals will recognize the unique talents present in the group and decide to resolve their conflicts, and jump in and tackle the task at hand. They will try to overcome their personal likes and dislikes of people in the group and work at accomplishing the task. Once again, if you practice patience, stay open, listen, try to praise fellow group members and acknowledge the contributions of every team member, a spirit of trust and deep respect will evolve. The facilitator's role is to reinforce the message that you don't have to like everyone, but you do need to learn to respect and work with them.

As soon as trust and respect are achieved, the group moves to the third stage, sometimes recognized as the *Norming Stage*. The members of the group begin to relax; they accept and respect the many different lenses through which their colleagues view the vision, and begin to work together toward consensus. There is an understanding and acceptance of the differences of opinions, and a sense of humor begins to evolve. Creativity abounds because everyone feels valuable, listened to, and accepted. We have a magnificent kaleidoscope of insights into the means of achieving the shared vision.

The final stage of team building is then called the *Performing Stage*. Once again we can compare this stage to that of an excellent orchestra. When an orchestra gives a superb performance, we know that each member of the group shows a high degree of mutual respect and trust. Each orchestra member is responsible for performing excellently with his or her own instrument, while complementing the performance of all the other players. At its best, an orchestra is a perfect example of the balance between *individual excellence* and *team harmony*. The result is beautiful music. When a group has a belief in synergy, a willingness to surrender territory and a built-in drive to put the shared vision and the success of the group above the needs of any one individual, the scene is set for excellent performance.

I personally experienced the trauma and value of team building during my term as the second president of Edison State College in New Jersey. When I took the position, it was during a time of great tension and stress. The college was ten years old and had experienced tremendous growth. In less than ten years, it had grown from a storefront enterprise to a college with more than three thousand students, a faculty, an administration, and a new headquarters.

Edison State is a very creative educational institution. It responds to the needs of adults who must work and take care of their families as well as pursue more education. To do this, it relies on a variety of delivery systems and has not developed a traditional campus. Courses are offered via computer, testing for credit, and other technologies. Because of this unique approach to education, the institution was suspect in the eyes of traditionalists.

The challenges were many! As one of the few women serving as state college presidents in the country, I felt vulnerable and extremely visible. I had taken the position as president because I strongly believed in the mission of the college. The first president had been a remarkable, visionary man. He gave birth to one of the most creative colleges of the decade. His talent was creativity. He was much less effective in dealing with people and organizing a rapidly growing institution. Now my challenge was to retain the creativity of the founder, but also deal with a poorly organized, demoralized staff, as well as a questioning, distrusting group of fellow presidents and faculty at the other New Jersey colleges.

I quickly recognized that I could not achieve all that needed to be done alone. The faculty, staff, administration, and I had to work together to establish a shared vision. There had to be a way to mobilize the energies of the staff of Edison to achieve this goal.

They were a bright, creative, committed group. Somehow I had to earn their trust and respect to make some much needed changes. They had to understand that it would take the hard work, talent, and motivation of everyone involved to achieve the status and recognition necessary to make the college a respected entity within New Jersey and nationally. One person with the title of president could never accomplish this goal.

I invited a friend and expert on visioning and team building to help us. He came to the college for several full-day intensive work and retreat sessions. At first there was grumbling and disinterest (typical of team-building stages one and two), but as the consultant skillfully worked, the group saw the value of what he was saying and began to contribute enthusiastically to the development of their teams. The more difficult step of getting the various teams to collaborate was yet to come (stage three).

I began to feel like an orchestra leader. Together we worked at weaving a shared vision. Each member began to contribute the excellence of his or her background and training. Creativity and energy were obvious to everyone who visited. By recommendation of the various teams, we reorganized the basic structure of the administration of the college. Leadership responsibility and authority were delegated to the various functional units. Every member of the college contributed his or her talents to achieving the goal of excellence. People in the state began to pay attention to what Edison State had to contribute. They recognized the value of this college to the adult learners needing education. Slowly but surely, Edison State was accepted as an equal partner among the nine state colleges of New Jersey. The faculty, staff, and administration were proud of what they had accomplished—together. Just as an orchestra is a perfect example of the balance between individual excellence and team harmony, the staff of Edison portrayed those same skills and the result in both cases is beautiful music.

I learned a great deal through this experience. I feared failure because the task seemed so immense and my visibility and vulnerability as the only woman state college president in New Jersey made me so obvious. I learned that the title of president was not the factor that led to success. I learned to see, hear, and feel the passion and needs of the staff. I learned the value of every voice, even though at times some of those voices seemed to be out of tune. I learned to delegate responsibility and authority and found that my trust in people was returned. *Creativity and trust abound when everyone feels valuable and accepted!*

Hannah Arendt said, "Power springs up when people act together; it vanishes the moment they disperse." [12] The strength of collaboration among the various constituencies—men and women, people of different cultures, people of different generations, people of different communities—will be reflected in the richness and success of their ventures. Like the contents of a kaleidoscope, they will come together to form beautiful images despite the differences of their points of view. No, this is not an easy task. It takes hard work and barrels of patience. However, the outcomes are worth the effort.

Chapter Seven

Practicing Effective Communication

Listening is more than a conflict management tool; it's the heart and soul of effective leadership.
—TERRY L. PAULSON

None of the achievements discussed in this book can be accomplished without excellent communication and listening abilities. Someone once said, "We rule the world by our words." I would add, and *with our ears*—by the power of our listening skills! There are some students of leadership who believe that all other aspects of effective leadership hinge on individuals' ability to communicate with meaning and to listen not only to what is being said, but to what is not being said—that is, to what is communicated by nonverbal cues. Let's look at a few examples of the different outcomes of good and poor communication.

Ty is the sales manager for a large recreational vehicle company in New York. One day, some of his staff informed him that his company had been receiving an increasing number of complaints about one of their new recreational vehicles. Ty decided to set up a hot line to receive the calls, and requested that all complaints be referred to him on a daily basis. He listened carefully and with full attention to the customers, and assured them that he wanted to hear their reports. He promised them that action would be taken and that the problems would be resolved. Because of his polite and concerned manner of communication and listening, most of the customers agreed to his recommendations for repairs and rebates.

After listening carefully to many calls, Ty was able to isolate three primary problems. He took the data to the engineers and tactfully communicated what he had heard on the hot line. He took care to be objective and professional in his delivery of the bad news. He had kept careful records of the complaints and was able to articulate them clearly. Naturally, the engineering department was upset by the number of complaints, but grateful for the way Ty had handled the problem. They immediately assigned a task force to reevaluate the product and discovered that Ty and the customers were correct.

Ty's ability to communicate and to listen to the customers saved the reputation of this company. His prompt action and manner of delivering the bad news to the engineering department could have caused conflict between sales and engineering design. However, his skillful communication—first with the customers and then with the engineers—served as a step to improved relations between the two departments. Ty exhibited excellence in two key leadership functions: communicating and listening.

Here is another example, but this example shows how easily we can miscommunicate. Cathy and Tim (not their real names) had worked well together for several years. They planned and implemented very complex seminars for potential community and academic leaders. These seminars were designed to be quite interactive and involved leaders from many different areas of the country. Cathy and Tim had an excellent track record. The seminars were well organized, flowed smoothly, and presented exciting experiences for the participants.

At one seminar in a new location, Tim indicated to Cathy that on the following day, the bus of participants should stop by one of the specialized schools in the area. Cathy, having had a long working relationship with Tim, assumed that this was a necessary change of plans and that Tim had made all the arrangements with the school. The next morning she called the school to remind them of the group's visit. The principal of the school was completely taken by surprise; she was totally unaware of the visit. She quickly called her teachers together, organized a reception committee, and prepared the teachers and students to meet the participants of the program.

What happened next was confusing and embarrassing to all parties involved. Tim was startled when the group got off the bus to visit the school. He questioned Cathy about this change in the schedule. She was confused and said, "You said we were supposed to 'stop by' here." Suddenly the reality of the miscommunication was clear to both of them. To Tim, "stop by" meant "stop the bus in front of the school" and share what is done at this particular school while the participants remained on the bus. To Cathy, "stop by" meant an actual quick visit to the school to observe the students and the teachers who worked there.

This miscommunication caused a great inconvenience to the principal and teachers at the school and was an embarrassment to both Cathy and Tim. Cathy should have questioned Tim about this sudden change in the agenda. Tim should have communicated his intentions more clearly and precisely to Cathy. In the stress of the responsibilities of the seminar, both individuals were listening and communicating in a distracted manner.

Sometimes miscommunication can have even more serious consequences. In the following example, all parties involved were seriously affected by the negative result. A very distracted truck dispatcher took a business message while chatting on another line with a friend. The message indicated that she was to send a truckload of produce to Portland. Intent on her conversation with her friend, she did not hear or bother to ask *which* Portland! She sent a truck full of fruit and vegetables to Portland, Oregon, instead of Portland, Maine, because she wasn't listening with full attention. What an embarrassing and costly error for the company! The company lost a lot of money and aggravated two long-term customers. Of course, it was costly to the dispatcher as well—she lost her job.

These examples exhibit the successes and failures that can be attributed to communication skills. It is almost impossible to function effectively as a leader without developing excellent communication and listening skills. Indeed, over the years I have come to the conclusion that the total effectiveness of leaders rises or falls in direct proportion to their ability to communicate with meaning, their interpersonal insights and actions, their willingness to enthusiastically share their goals and vision, and their willingness *to be active, positive listeners.*

The Meaning of Communication

Regardless of the dictionary definition of communication, I agree with Joe Batten, the author of *Tough-Minded Leadership,* when he says that we can define communication in four words: *shared meaning, shared understanding.* These four words really say it all. Is there anything more we need for a successful relationship? For a successful career? For a successful family life?[1] Aren't these four words the key to weaving a shared vision? They are certainly the means to understanding and accepting different points of view as we develop teams for collaborative action. These four words are the foundation of the concepts of servant leadership (the understanding that to lead is to serve) reflected in everything we have said about leadership so far. To have shared meaning and shared understanding, we must develop ourselves to be service oriented, vulnerable, open, caring—and, of course, positive, active listeners.

It takes real courage and patience to become and remain open and vulnerable in our relationships and communication with others. Sometimes it would be so much easier if we could just tell people what to do and then expect it to be done—or better yet, just do it ourselves. However, communicating in an open, honest fashion is the only way to cultivate an environment that fosters a spirit of trust and love. I think we all recognize that without trust, an environment can quickly become a very uncomfortable place to be. Paranoia and suspicion run rampant, and very little movement toward a common goal is accomplished.

Through openness, we position ourselves to better understand the other person's perspective, and not judge it as right or wrong but merely *different.* It takes a genuine, humble leader to be able to say, "What a great idea! I didn't see it that way, but it just might work better than what I was proposing" or "Tell me more about your idea; it is totally foreign to my experience and I'd like to hear more about it." This openness is an essential element to communicating with meaning and actively listening—two characteristics critical to developing a shared vision and a trusting environment.

As a leader, in addition to being open, it is also important to be prepared to communicate your ideas in a clear and organized fashion, and to anticipate that others may make suggestions that will enhance those ideas. Show by your words and by your behavior that you are open to these enhancements. Unless people see and feel that their ideas are part of the vision and they are part of the excitement of making something happen, they won't care much about the outcomes. When information is shared rather than guarded, people feel included and respected and will put their energy into making whatever it is a success. Shared meaning and shared understanding help everyone comprehend the reasons behind decisions, and also help them see how they are linked to the shared vision, values, and common purpose.

Raydean Acevedo, president of Research Management Consultants, Inc. (RMCI), holds open strategy sessions at her company to share information. Instead of executive sessions for a small group of top administrators to develop strategies based on a closed agenda, she holds open meetings on a regular basis and allows a larger group of employees to develop and help choose alternatives. As a result, all the employees believe that they are a part of the decision-making process, that they have been involved in developing the plans. They are then committed to the goals and give 150 percent of their energies to make the company a success. Communication and feedback are at the heart of effective leadership. Raydean said, "I attribute the success of RMCI to the environment of trust, compassion, and love which has evolved among all of us. Open communication in times of great stress as well as the good times has helped establish this environment."[2]

The smartest policy is to share with others everything you possibly can—give them all the information they might need to know. Keep them so well supplied with correct information that they trust you, and rumors won't have a chance to get a foothold. Once a decision has been made about anything, the wisest course is to announce it as fast as you can—before the rumor mill beats you to it.

Convinced? Or Just Stubborn?

As you get to know yourself and your passion, and as you begin to practice the skills necessary for effective leadership, you will gain a new sense of self-confidence. Self-confident persons usually hold very strong opinions. Their communications tend to be forceful and persuasive because they believe in them so completely. However, a narrow-minded self-confidence that becomes self-righteous and excludes the opinions of others is egocentric and certainly not service oriented. In fact, the person whose constant concern is to maintain the rightness of one point of view may in truth be insecure and defensive rather than self-confident. These folks don't get very far very fast because they turn people off instead of turning them on. Instead of drawing people to their point of view, they tend to drive them away.

Think about it—most of us know that defensive, closed-minded people plateau early in their careers or community activity. They are so busy stubbornly defending their point of view, their opinion, that they have no time to become a part of a group that is developing a shared vision for the future. These are the folks who are derailed. They are so busy listening to themselves that they never hear the roar of the crowd as it passes them by!

Leaders cannot afford to exhibit what others might interpret as stubbornness or unwillingness to listen to different points of view. Neither can they expect to be successful if they convey their message with incomplete, mixed, or unclear communication in behavior or words.

Communication Barriers

Let's spend some time discussing a few of the more obvious communication barriers. Words alone have very little meaning outside their dictionary definition. Words are really a means to an end; they are the vehicles for the expression of the thoughts and feelings of the persons using them. When we speak, we send a message both verbally and nonverbally. The message evolves from our base of experience. It reflects our attitude, our expectations, our values, our feelings, our knowledge and intelligence, and sometimes even our needs and motivation. Our instructions—our words and the way we deliver them—can create an environment of trust and creativity or one of suspicion and distrust.

Our language, or the way we use words, can sometimes pose a barrier to good communication. For example, do you pepper your conversations with jargon originating from your training or background? Do you frequently use alphabet soup when talking about organizations or products unfamiliar to your listeners, forcing people to ask for clarification? We need to be sensitive to the group or individual we are working with and communicate with them in such a way that we trigger their interest, their desire to understand and participate. Remember the case of Cathy and Tim? Their interpretations of the phrase "stop by" were entirely different. We need to do our best to know and understand the possible interpretations of what we are saying. We can't be paranoid and worry about every word we utter, but we should be knowledgeable enough to discern the confusing nature of some statements or the possible inflammatory connotations of others.

Mumblers or speed speakers tax everyone's patience. It is very annoying to be repeatedly forced to ask a person to restate something. It is even more aggravating to have to ask for clarification three or four times in one conversation. Do you talk so fast that some words and meaning are lost? Clarity of diction and a proper tone of voice are within almost everyone's reach. It simply takes practice, consideration for the listener, self-confidence, and a desire to convey a message.

Your tone of voice also conveys additional (and sometimes opposing) meaning to your message. Your voice can send a message of insistence, questioning, whining, demanding, anger, or pleading. Try saying the following sentence in each of the different tones listed above: "Can you do something about the noise level in this room?" Notice, it can be a question, an exclamation, a statement, or a plea. It can be delivered as a monotone or your voice can be full of enthusiasm. Add facial expressions and hand movements to your delivery and you will note a striking difference each time you say it. Now, stand in front of a mirror and experiment with the following statement: "Our community center must have $200,000 and it is up to us to raise it." What do you notice about your delivery? Is it easier for you to be a grumbler or a motivator? What is your style of communication? Does it need to improve? How?

Have you ever tried to listen to a person who always speaks in a quiet monotone? Were you able to pay attention? Did this person capture your imagination? Even though the person may be very intelligent and have good ideas, if the voice lacks energy and conviction, people will not take the words seriously. Dull delivery tends to put you into a sound sleep!

What are your speech habits? Tape record yourself. Do you like what you hear? Have someone else videotape you during a presentation or while you are conducting a committee meeting. Play it back and take note of your strengths and what needs to be improved. The tone of your voice is a very, very important part of your ability to generate enthusiasm and involvement or negativism and boredom.

Nonverbal cues also confirm or deny the message you are attempting to send with your words and tone of voice. Nonverbal cues are messages sent by the speaker's gestures, facial expressions, eyes, and posture. Other people interpret what you have to say by using their ears, their eyes, their past experience, and their intuition. Some communication experts say that more than half of our human interaction is through nonverbal communication. If you have the courage to have someone videotape you, take a look at your body language—your nonverbal cues. Do they change the reality of your message? How did your audience respond to you? What can you do to become a better communicator?

According to Warren Bennis and Burt Nanus, "Communication creates meaning for people. Or should. It's the only way any group, small or large, can become aligned behind the [shared] goals of an organization."[3] Getting the message across to everyone on every level is an absolute key to success. "Basically it is what the creative process is all about and what . . . separates the managers from the leaders."[4]

Your attitude can either facilitate communication or stop it short. As mentioned earlier, being so highly opinionated that you refuse to listen to the ideas of others is a sure trip to doomed communication. Losing your temper is another quick turn-off. People resent a hothead. They tend to ignore the message and focus on the unpleasantness of the personality. If you are attempting to weave a shared vision or move an organization or community to a new level of excellence, it can only be accomplished with patience, love, and understanding, not with anger, shouting, or forced action.

Deborah Doxtator told me about an example of the result of impatience. At one point in her career as Oneida Tribal Chairwoman, Deborah lost patience and had a heated confrontation with a staff person. This rather young, inexperienced staff member had all the potential to develop into an excellent leader for the tribe and looked up to Deborah as a mentor and role model. The confrontation with Deborah was a very demoralizing and intimidating factor in her life. She lost self-confidence and became even more timid. Deborah considers her impatience and this emotional confrontation one of the serious mistakes in her career. Deborah said, "I felt that I wasn't in the right because I didn't give her the affirmation that she needed when she needed it. In order to be a leader, we have to be positive and patient in the relationships we have with those we work with."

Electronic communications can prove to be a marvelous tool or another excuse to avoid dealing with people on a face-to-face basis. The use of e-mail and the Internet to give prompt responses to others without infringing on their time or wasting our own precious time by frequent unanswered phone calls is invaluable. However, sending an e-mail message to a person working in the office on the other side of the wall or living in the house next door detracts from the possible evolution of the shared meaning and shared understanding that are so essential to true communication. Try to choose the right medium at the right time. Sometimes a warm smile and face-to-face communication are essential, at others e-mail or a letter will be perfectly satisfactory. It is up to you to intuitively and sensitively understand the impact of your choice. Just as leadership and followership can be thought of as the two sides of a single sheet of paper, communicating your thoughts and listening to others should be thought of as two inseparable skills.

Key Elements of Listening

"Hear what a person wants to say, what he doesn't want to say, and what he is unable to say without help."[5]

I can't talk about the tools of communication without also discussing *listening*. Have you ever caught yourself gazing intently at a speaker, but realizing that you haven't heard a word for the last several minutes? Did you formulate an opinion long before the person had completed the message? And while the person was speaking, were you preparing precisely what you were going to say in reply instead of listening? Both listeners and speakers build behaviors or create filters that either help or hinder the communication process. Just as body language and attitude affect your manner of delivering a message, they also affect the manner in which you receive a message.

The dispatcher in the example I shared with you earlier was more interested in listening to the chit-chat from her friend than to the message from her boss. She was distracted and failed to hear the complete message, so she made a major error. There are also times when we really don't want to hear the message, so we tune out the speaker. That is *negative listening*. Sometimes husbands and wives, parents and children, or students and teachers slip into this listening style. We may give the person the time to present the message, we hear them out, but then we say exactly what we were going to say in the first place—in other words, we listen but we don't really hear at all.

Or what about *selective listening?* Sometimes we can listen to only what we want to hear and then ignore the rest of the person's statement. This style of listening is like an antenna, tuned to listen in a particular way, somewhat like radar. "Radar is an antenna that is very selective: it locates solid objects. . . . Radar picks up only what it is designed to pick up."[6] Like radar, selective listening picks up only what we want to hear. "It acts as a filter that rejects what does not 'fit' the current paradigm [of our thinking], or shapes the input so that it does fit."[7] Therefore, if we want to learn or create something new, or keep something in place that we believe is most effective, and someone says something that doesn't fit with what we already are convinced is right, it does not register on our radar.[8] We simply don't hear it!

Positive listening must be much more than an act or pose. The person who cultivates the style of communicating with meaning also develops a genuine desire to know what other people are really thinking, saying, and feeling. Listening itself can be a very clear means of communicating important feelings and attitudes to others. The manner in which you listen conveys a variety of important things to the person speaking to you. For example, your manner of listening may communicate:

- That you believe what the person has to say is important
- That you are interested in the individual as a unique human being

- That you may not agree with the speaker, but you understand the rationale and realize that it is valid in its own terms
- That the person is someone who is worth listening to and that you are open to new and different ideas

All these factors are important, but perhaps the most important reason for cultivating a positive listening style is that it serves as a means of establishing trust in a relationship. Without trust, very little real progress can be made toward achieving a shared vision.

I am aware of a situation where the person in charge consistently swivels his chair so that his back is to the speakers if he is uncomfortable with the message they are bringing to him. This has a different effect on the speakers depending on their self-confidence and the security they feel in their positions. Some are deeply intimidated; others become insulted and very angry. They all feel that their ideas are not being heard or are not acceptable to this person.

Barriers to Positive Listening

Your listening style can serve as a bridge or a barrier to good communication. Let's talk about some of the possible barriers to positive listening and reflect on how to avoid them.

Probably the most difficult person to communicate with is the daydreamer. Have you ever tried to carry on a meaningful conversation with a person who has that far-away look in his or her eyes? Have you felt as though someone is present but not really there? Have you felt nervous and tense because of someone's fidgeting or distraction? How does this behavior affect your ability to communicate? Of course, it is a real turn-off! Sometimes the only way to get people's attention is to talk about *their* interests. When I have experienced this listening behavior, I have fluctuated between two emotions: anger and frustration. Neither of these emotions is very helpful to developing a trusting relationship or communicating clearly. How can we correct this listening style?

First of all, if you are guilty of being a daydreamer, try concentrating on what other people have to say even if it doesn't happen to be your favorite topic. Second, keep eye contact; this will help to control distractions and focus on the message of the person who is speaking. Sometimes this may require some patience, but in the long run, it may bring you some new, creative ideas and confirm a loyal bond with the person involved. Third, deal with the possibility that your daydreaming response is physiological. Do you set up meetings at a time of the day when you are exhausted? If this is the case, change your meeting times, or if your energy is low all day long, seek the advice of your physician; you may have an easily remedied physical problem.

Another negative listening style involves jumping to conclusions. If you develop this sort of reputation, your colleagues will be turned off before they even begin to communicate. Someone who jumps to conclusions always seems to have all the answers before anyone has the chance to talk about the problem. Coworkers feel cornered when they must deliver a message in the face of a judgmental, critical, and know-it-all attitude. *Patience, patience, patience, and humility* are the answers to correcting this listening style. Remember, no one has all the answers, so wait and listen to the ideas of others.

It is amazing how frequently we will hear an idea that is far better than our own, or that richly embellishes our own, if we listen positively and without the need to defend the purity of our own position. Also, by cultivating positive listening, we enhance the possibility of getting to know and understand the perspectives, needs, and cultures of our various team members.

According to Roger Fritz in *You're in Charge,* business people and other professionals are said to devote seven of their ten working hours daily to either communicating or receiving information. Of this time, writing accounts for 11 percent; reading consumes up to 15 percent; talking takes another 31 percent; and listening demands 43 percent. Is there any question concerning the vital role listening and communication play in leadership growth and development?[9]

Entire books have been written about communication and listening. You may want to review a few of them if you feel that further insight will help you in your goal of becoming a more effective leader. If you don't want to read an entire book on the subject, at least take the time to honestly reflect on your listening style. What kind of a listener are you? Rushed? Thoughtful? Critical? Distracted? How well does your style contribute to your overall success in your community? In your personal life? At your work?

Most people believe they are effective listeners. However, much of the time we only assume the posture of listening. Just because we have ears, we think we are listening. In a sense that is like saying that just because we have eyes, we can read. We all know that the latter is certainly not true. Undiagnosed bad listening habits such as interrupting, daydreaming, jumping to conclusions, listening selectively, or showing boredom prevent us from becoming capable, effective leaders. The only way to progress is to make some conscious decisions to discover our limitations and then try to change.

A friend of mine, Perry Smith (who is also an expert on leadership development), uses an excellent metaphor when he talks about listening. He points out that when we want to see something better we sometimes squint—therefore, if we want to hear something better, perhaps we should squint with our ears.[10] The first time I heard this statement it made me smile, but it certainly conveys the message that we should try harder to hear what the other person has to say.

As is true with most behavior, communicating with meaning and positive listening are contagious. If a person displays skillful, inclusive communication and listening skills, these qualities are generally adopted throughout the organization. An open, trusting environment begins to evolve.

Communication and Trust

Gus Garcia is a city councilman in Austin, Texas. He firmly believes that service to the people is the highest honor that a person can achieve. His family has been involved in service leadership positions for more than 250 years. Gus has been very successful. In addition to serving as a councilman, he hosts a television talk show that encourages the citizens to speak their minds on the many critical issues facing the community, and he is also involved in numerous other community activities.

Gus told me that because he is highly visible and very open about what he values, he frequently gets himself into trouble. By speaking openly and honestly about difficult issues in the community, he sometimes steps on people's toes. However, he does not allow friendship or personality to get in the way of his integrity and ethical decision making. He insists on open lines of communication. He refuses to have his phone calls screened because he believes that it is his responsibility to listen—according to Gus, "A leader must always be accessible."

On one occasion, after visiting several neighborhoods, Gus persuaded and led the city council in the establishment of a curfew ordinance for one of the neighborhoods in southeast Austin. The American Civil Liberties Union and people from all other areas of the city rose up in protest. They accused Gus of infringing on the rights of the people. They accused him of betraying his own people. What they didn't know was that Gus had listened, investigated, researched the issue, and communicated with the people of this southeast Austin neighborhood. The decision for the curfew did not come from Gus, it came from the people of the neighborhood! This is what *they* wanted and they had come to Gus because they trusted him, believed in him, and knew that he would listen to them and not betray them. No amount of bullying from special interest groups could divert Gus from responding to the needs of the people.

Gus has established a reputation as a listener, a communicator, a person of integrity. He said, "Even though some of the people may disagree with me, they do not ever question my integrity and my dedication to duty. I have been clear on where I stand on ethics and values. I feel that I am not going to lose friends because they understand why I do what I do. Even though we disagree, they still respect my opinion."

Gus clearly understands that one of the responsibilities of leadership is to communicate, to listen, to collaborate, and to form trusting relationships. Of course, none of these tools of good communication can ensure excellent communication unless you are recognized as a person of integrity. Without integrity, there is no credibility, no trust; and without credibility and trust there is no true communication. People may listen to your directives and follow you because they must or because they have no other alternative, but they will not recognize you as their true leader. When the going gets tough, they will be gone very quickly.

Trust is fragile. It is extremely important to maintain, extremely easy to lose, and very, very hard to win back. Trust is the glue that binds team members together. Trust is the ingredient that serves as the basis for a leader's legitimacy. Trust cannot be bought or sold; it must be earned. Ethics and integrity in what you say and what you do are the key to creating a lasting sense of purpose that can earn credibility and trust.

Unless your words and actions consistently reflect your values and your decisions are made with a sense of integrity and dependability, there can be no trust. Excellent communication and active listening can form a firm foundation for the development of trusting relationships. All your actions and decisions should be consistent with your stated intentions and with the highest standards of ethics and integrity. Don't be afraid to be yourself! Saying what you believe in an objective, open, honest, nonpersonal way quickly eliminates suspicion and paranoia. It is perhaps one of the best-kept secrets of being an effective leader.

Chapter Eight

Deciding How to Decide

*Every decision is a statement, even those decisions you
don't intend as such. Some are statements to the masses.
Some are statements to a few. All are statements to and
about yourself.*
—HAP KLOPP

I have a very close friend who sends me into a tailspin whenever he
has to make a decision. He either avoids making the decision completely or goes into a series of statements such as, "I really don't care;
do whatever you'd like," or he questions his decision incessantly
with, "What do you think?" . . . "Are you sure this is all right?" . . .
"Should we ask someone if this is suitable?" Of course, I usually do
what I know I shouldn't! I impatiently make the decision myself.
This does nothing to help him become a better decision maker, but
my impatience gets the better of me.

Decision making, like all other leadership skills, takes practice.
But before we can practice, we need to develop some understanding of the importance of establishing an acceptable style of decision making. Yes, persons who assume the leadership role must
also assume the responsibility for setting the tone of the organization, the spirit of the team, and the styles of decision making. In
fact, perhaps one of the most important decisions a new organization or leader must make is deciding how to decide! Unfortunately,
this crucial determination is frequently overlooked or made in
haste when a critical issue involving great risk is at hand.

Communication, active listening, and the values and culture of
the organization or community all play a part in the determination

of a style of decision making. The style of decision making in turn plays an important part in the development of group culture. One feeds the other. As I have said, shaping a culture in which group members can trust each other enough to work together toward a common goal is one of the most important leadership tasks. It creates the environment in which each individual can become fully committed to the shared vision, and to the important part each person must play to make it happen. If this trusting environment exists, then the style of decision making becomes inconsequential because there is an openness and understanding of what must be done to accomplish the vision.

In the past, traditional theorists in schools of business have talked about decision making in terms of a multistep process. First, identify the problem; second, identify possible solutions; third, make a decision about how to arrive at which solution to choose (decide how to decide); fourth, select a solution; fifth, make and then evaluate the decision. This is a very rational, orderly model of decision making, but do we always have the luxury of time to think through these precise steps? Hardly! Most decisions are made in a much more automatic and intuitive fashion. It is a rare individual who follows the theoretical step-by-step process. So don't be deceived; there is no one perfect style or form of decision making. There is no perfect formula that can be used in every organization or community all the time.

Some authors may strongly advocate one or another style; however, I believe that decision-making methods need to vary. The style selected will depend on the level of involvement of those persons who will be directly affected by the decision, and on the sophistication and confidence of the person who is ultimately responsible for the outcomes of the decision. I've said it before and I will repeat it again, *all* people must be respected for the various talents they bring to the organization. Once they have discovered their passion and found their voice, their energy and commitment will be contagious. However, this does not mean that every person in the organization must be involved in every decision to be made. The principal of the school doesn't need to be involved in decisions about the menu for the school lunches. Nor does the cook need to be part of the decision-making process concerning the school curriculum. A surgeon is responsible for the decisions he makes in the operating room, but it is not his prerogative to make the decisions about where to order the supplies. Each of these individuals would be wasting time and energy thinking about issues that are in someone else's area of expertise.

Strive always to push decision making to the level where it should most properly occur. The leaders we need in our communities for the future are leaders who know how to share power, and who back the decisions of their team members firmly, consistently, and fairly. They can then fully expect that the team members will provide the same type of support to them when it is needed. They recognize that today they lead and tomorrow they follow.

The leader who understands sharing and collaboration, and who respects the capabilities and strengths of everyone involved, will carefully consider the appropriateness of all possibilities and forms of the decision-making style spectrum. That is, they will involve everyone in shaping the decision, or they will involve an internal committee, or one or more outside experts, or at the other extreme, they will involve no one. Their ability to openly and honestly communicate the reason they chose to include or exclude others in the decision-making process is the key to the acceptability of any style, and to the maintenance or establishment of trust.

Styles of Decision Making

People who believe that their voice is heard—and that it is considered important—will accept the different styles of decision making that the leader may choose. No single method of decision making is the perfect one for all times and places; the appropriate one to use depends on the situation. Let's review some of the optional styles for making decisions. Decisions can be made by:

- A single person, without input from anyone else
- A single person, with solicited input from others
- A person designated as an expert on the question being considered
- A majority vote
- A consensus

If a leader wants personal or organizational support in making a decision, he or she should solicit as much participation as possible.

Asking for the participation of others when faced with an important decision usually sends a message of your personal philosophy about people. It implies a deep respect and understanding of the diversity of talents to be found within any organization or community. Having said this, I also acknowledge that it requires a great deal of patience. It usually takes more time and energy to reach agreement when many persons are involved, but the extra time and effort are often offset by the goodwill and effectiveness with which the decision will be implemented. When people are involved in the decision-making process, they have a better understanding of why the decision was made, and can be expected to be more committed to the decision and its outcomes than if the decision had been made by a single person seen as the leader.

During my presidency at Edison State, I was faced with some difficult budgetary decisions. A balanced budget was the mandate for every college in the state of New Jersey. I knew that some drastic steps would have to be taken if we were to achieve this goal. It was also evident to me that if I made the necessary budgetary cuts unilaterally, I would risk losing the support of the faculty and staff. I decided to involve the entire staff in the decision-making process.

The administrative team of the college was very apprehensive about this decision. They were afraid that if everyone were aware of the limited budget for the new fiscal year, it would cause departmental conflicts and leave the staff fearful and demoralized. Reality indicated that they could be right. The risk was apparent, but I decided to adhere to my decision to involve everyone.

We scheduled a full staff and faculty meeting. We shared the state of the budget with the group and asked for their recommendations for cuts and revisions. The experience was exhilarating. The group responded with keen insight and sensitivity. They basically made all the recommendations we needed. In addition, they offered us some excellent ideas that the administrative team and I had never thought of during our confidential strategy sessions.

The risk of sharing the information and decision making was great, but in my mind the risk of losing the support and trust of the college community by a unilateral approach to the problem was even greater. We achieved our goal of a balanced budget, and the entire staff and faculty shared in the pride of having accomplished this very difficult task.

In this situation, I used three different forms of decision making. First of all, I sought the advice of the vice presidents concerning a procedure to achieve a balanced budget. Their recommendations were to keep these very important decisions within the confines of the confidentiality of the Administrative Council. These recommendations were politely rejected. After careful consideration of the risks, I unilaterally made the decision to share all the information with the total college faculty and staff. Admittedly, intuition rather than common sense led me to this decision. The process of decision making that we then followed was totally participative and based on a consensus model. All three of these decisions were based on the situation and need, so all were acceptable.

It is not surprising to note that the consensus method is most effective when the group has reached the stage of development where individual differences are not only tolerated, but welcomed, and there is a high level of trust. We talked about this in Chapter Six, when we discussed the great value of staying open to a variety of opinions and points of view. I decided to trust the talented, committed faculty and staff of Edison and counted on their thoughtful insight. They lived up to my expectations!

By now you must certainly see the close relationships among the factors characterizing the essence of effective leadership. Whether it is weaving a shared vision, being open to many points of view, learning to communicate, or making decisions, respect for the dignity and worth of every individual involved is the critical ingredient.

However, there are those situations when the participative style of decision making is not appropriate. Imagine the waste of time incurred by having everyone decide where to purchase supplies or when to approve vacations or make appointments. Neither would it be appropriate for some even more important decisions such as the hiring and firing of personnel or salary increases for various personnel. It is also not appropriate when group members lack relevant expertise, or when implementation does not require full cooperation. In these situations, it is more appropriate to use one of the less time-consuming methods.

Eleanor Josaitis, a talented woman and cofounder of FOCUS: HOPE in Detroit, shared a decision-making dilemma that reflects the essential nature of sometimes calling upon outside experts. FOCUS: HOPE is an organization pledged to intelligent and practical action to overcome racism, poverty, and injustice and to build a metropolitan community where people of every creed and color may live in freedom, harmony, trust, and affection. When the manufacturing industry began moving out of Detroit, Eleanor and Father Bill Cunningham, an activist and parish priest, decided to purchase one of the deserted buildings. Their dream was to start a technology training center for inner-city youth. Neither Eleanor nor Father Bill had any knowledge of the manufacturing process; they just had a dream. Eleanor laughingly told us that as she, her husband, and Father Bill walked through the deserted building, dreaming about what could be accomplished there, her husband turned to Father Bill and said, "I hope you know what you're talking about because I guarantee you, she doesn't!"

Eleanor told us that her salvation has been her willingness to surround herself with people who understood the manufacturing process. She was never embarrassed to call on outside experts for advice and help. She has even succeeded in co-opting some of these experts to volunteer their services to assist with the training at FOCUS: HOPE.

This is an intriguing example because Eleanor, who has no knowledge of technology, has energetically assumed a leadership role in the development of the technology center of FOCUS: HOPE. She has done this by sharing the vision, empowering others to act, and maintaining a strong sense of values and openness. Yes, she has lobbied Congress, she has persuaded the large corporations to donate equipment, time, and expertise, but primarily Eleanor has counted on and valued the expertise of other people. Eleanor firmly believes that people want to be invited to be part of the solution in addressing any problem. She is an extraordinary example of a leader who understands that leadership means service, that the authoritarian model of leadership is rarely effective, and that being open to many points of view strengthens her leadership! She operates efficiently in all styles of decision making and never hesitates to acknowledge that someone else might know more than she does about a certain topic. Not everyone will find this model comfortable. Many of us will need to continue learning about developing our flexibility as we become more skilled in the practice of leadership.

Seeking the advice of an outside expert is becoming more necessary as we operate in a rapidly changing society. It is almost impossible for everyone to stay abreast of all the most current information. Reaching out to experts who have chosen to specialize in a segment of the flood of information may be a wise decision. Don't anticipate that everyone in your organization or community will be happy with decisions recommended by a committee or an expert. There is always the possibility of offending someone in the organization who may be able to offer the same or better expertise than the outside expert. Still, most groups and organizations respond well if they know that in most cases the leader will seek out and recognize relevant expertise within the organization before looking for outside experts.

The decision to seek expertise within the organization first can be a very strong step toward the development of a culture of trust. By soliciting information or advice from a colleague or team member, you are sending a message to everyone indicating your respect and knowledge of the expertise of all individuals involved in the project or community.

Yes, every decision leads us somewhere—that somewhere may be a positive leap toward group cohesiveness or a step in the wrong direction. As we noted at the start of this chapter, Hap Klopp, president of North Face, the world's leading manufacturer of outdoor adventure equipment, has observed: "Every decision is a statement, even those decisions you don't intend as such. Some are statements to the masses. Some are statements to a few. All are statements to and about yourself."[1]

Klopp tells the story of being hired to turn around a failing business, the Ski Hut. During his first week he decided to spend his time walking around and looking at the physical facilities. One of the first things he noticed was that the warehouse was in chaos. He determined that it was in as bad condition as the accounting process, if not worse. He decided to tackle the warehouse problem first. This may seem strange, but his rationale was that if you couldn't find the products the customers were ordering, you couldn't respond to customer requests, and so you certainly couldn't make sales. No wonder the business was floundering!

He immediately made a *unilateral decision* that may have appeared to be another odd decision for a new manager. He decided to personally spend two days of hard labor in the warehouse with some of the staff. Together, they completely reorganized the warehouse for easy access. Amazing as it may seem, this decision was his first step toward turning around the failing company. He knew that by making the decision to do physical labor in the warehouse first, he was setting an example. His decision made a statement to all the employees. His actions showed the employees that he was not afraid of hard work, that satisfying requests from customers was his highest priority, and that he believed in organization and efficiency. He then fired the warehouse manager, which sent the message that he was serious. The employees also discovered that he understood how business really works—he made the warehouse his first priority and then tackled the accounting system. The troops rallied around him and in one year they had turned the business completely around.[2]

It is very important to understand the importance of every decision that you make as a leader. Each decision will affect people, it will communicate your values, it will symbolize your understanding of the whole and your willingness to share or clutch power. It will serve as the strongest indicator of your respect for the expertise available among your team members.

The story of Gus Garcia in Chapter Seven is another excellent example of a different style of decision making. That example shows the actions of a single person making a decision after *soliciting input from others*. After seeking the opinions of all the people in a particular neighborhood, he made the decision to push the resolution for a curfew for that neighborhood through the city council. He didn't make that decision alone, nor did he ask the advice of an outside expert. He held the elected position to act, but he first looked for recommendations from the people who would be affected, then he used his power and influence to make their desire a reality. He convinced the other members of the city council to vote for the resolution. This was a three-step process:

- First, he listened to the recommendations of the neighborhood people who would be affected.
- Second, he decided they knew what was best for them.
- Third, he persuaded others to vote for what the people wanted.

This was a time-consuming activity, but it gained further respect and loyalty for Gus.

Some persons in leadership positions find it easier to always choose the authoritative model for making decisions. The excuse for using only this method of decision making is that it eliminates the possibility of conflict. This is far from the truth! Conflicts are unavoidable in human relations. They are either hidden behind closed doors, or open, healthy, creative differences of opinion. A healthy approach to conflict is one that makes use of it as a means of building trust, creating innovative solutions to problems, and strengthening relationships. But unless serious attention is given to addressing conflicts constructively, the opposite may occur, generating distrust, destroying relationships, and stifling creativity. Conflicts that remain under the surface tend to erupt in very unpredictable and destructive ways.

In an organization that is functioning effectively, leadership is a shared responsibility. That means decision making is also a shared responsibility, and that a level of trust exists that allows the method of decision making to vary according to the circumstances, the persons involved, and the issue at hand. Leadership for the future will develop and encourage the concept of the team. The leader's actions will reflect an understanding that leaders do not exist without followers and that followers are the designators of leaders.

The person acting as leader will always be there to assist the team by facilitating problem solving and conflict resolution, and by celebrating the completion of each step toward the shared vision and goals of the organization. If you agree that service is a primary function of leadership, then understanding the process by which a group becomes most responsive to working together and solving difficulties is an essential quality of this service.

Styles of decision making, risk taking, team building, conflict resolution—all this sounds like a lot of work! It is, indeed, a tremendous amount of work. It can be very frustrating for persons who consider themselves to be visionary leaders to focus on process. However, getting to know who your colleagues are, how you relate to each other, and how you work together in arriving at decisions is the most effective way to build and sustain an organization as a community.

Do you dislike making decisions? Are you like the friend I spoke of at the beginning of this chapter? Are you always ready to let someone else make the decision for you? Do you then complain about the decisions that are made? Well, even if you don't make a decision, you've made a decision. You decided *not* to decide! Just because you stand still doesn't mean the world does; time marches on at its steady pace. If a deadline is approaching and your mind is stuck in the muck of indecision, time seems to move even faster. When a crisis occurs, there is very little time to spend in analysis. It is time for action. The consequences of indecision can be enormous. Worst of all, it isn't always a sudden catastrophe; frequently it is a slow death, decades of misery contemplating what might have been, had you only made a decision! Decision making takes practice. Each new decision, whether it is viewed as good or bad, provides opportunities for risk taking and new learning. As with many other processes, practice makes perfect.

Ethics, Values, and Decision Making

The values and ethics reflected in the decisions and the style of making the decisions also have a powerful and lasting effect on the values and ethics of the organization. For example, if trust is an important value, then the style of decision making chosen is important because it can serve as a means of establishing a trusting environment.

According to *Merriam-Webster's Collegiate Dictionary*, ethics is defined as "a set of moral principles or values";[3] it relates to what is right or wrong, good or bad. However, when it comes to decision making, the right thing isn't always easy to discern. We all want to do what is right, but good intentions frequently get lost among complex issues, personal conflicts, demands of those above us in an organization, or competitive pressures. For example, what would you do in the following situation?

Let's suppose that your organization had been receiving a number of bomb threats. You are the person to whom fifteen other people report. When the first call comes in to the switchboard, you don't even think twice; your decision is to evacuate the building. The police and the fire department are called and everyone is relieved when nothing is found. Then the calls begin to come in on a daily basis—four days in a row you have evacuated the building. You thank God that none of the calls have revealed a bomb; they are all hoaxes. However, the disruption of the work schedule is beginning to take its toll on productivity and order. The fifth day there is no bomb threat and work goes on in a positive but somewhat apprehensive fashion. On the sixth day, the calls begin again! You find yourself facing a dilemma. *There is a deadline to meet, and all the previous calls have proved to be false. What would you do?* Evacuate the building again? Ignore the call and don't tell anyone about it? Notify the police and the staff and leave the decision to evacuate or stay on the job to each individual?

Take some time to reflect on the above scenario. Talk it over with a friend. Indeed, decision making is not always quick and easy—it is frequently a complex dilemma!

Persons who assume a leadership role have a responsibility to provide their team or community with a clear statement of policies and values. Otherwise, the lack of such a statement might itself provide a rationale for undesirable behavior by team members—perhaps without their even forming a conscious conclusion. Even parents can send a message to their children that can be easily misconstrued. For example, an inordinate amount of pressure on bringing home an A grade can send the additional hidden message of "at any cost." Then cheating on exams or finding other devious means of achieving an A becomes acceptable behavior in the minds of the children. They are meeting the bottom line of the values expressed by their parents. Each decision is made not on moral grounds, but on the degree to which it furthers the objectives of achieving the A to satisfy what they perceive as their parents' bottom line.

At other times, people may be led to unethical decisions by individuals who hold a position that allows them to act as role models, supervisors, or coaches. *Ethics: Easier Said Than Done* quotes an English teacher—coach for the outstanding, academically victorious Steinmetz High School academic team in Chicago—as saying to the students entrusted to his care, "Everybody cheats. That's the way the world works." The article continues, "According to a team member, [this teacher's] sage advice also included: '[You're] fools just to play by the rules.'"[4]

This man's moral counsel led the students to a dubious victory in statewide competition, then to embarrassment and condemnation when the team's widespread cheating was revealed. Even when it was obvious that the cheating had been exposed, this teacher had one more morsel of bad advice to give to the students as they were called in for questioning: "Give the performance of [your] lives."⁵ Sadly, such unethical, valueless behavior is frequently found in our competitive society. But blaming others will not correct this unethical behavior—rather, modeling behavior that portrays leadership as ethical, caring, compassionate, and respectful can serve as a powerful force for change.

Miriam and Kenneth Clark, in *Choosing to Lead*, tell us that sometimes "extraneous issues are ignored in the pursuit of single-minded goals. So employees in the tobacco industry believe in and participate in launching advertising campaigns for cigarettes to increase market share, even when the campaign targets young people or people of developing countries; a college makes unrealistic promises to outstanding faculty or students it wishes to recruit; a political party sets a platform that cannot be actualized, promising benefits to constituents that cannot be fulfilled. Some writers compare organizational behavior to chess: 'It is all a game, the rules are known, do anything to win.'"⁶

"Do anything to win" is not a framework within which I recommend decision making or action. The ethics and values that are supposed to distinguish human beings from other forms of life are wisdom, courage, reverence, love, compassion, kindness, peace, and gratitude. If this is true, then our decisions should reflect more than doing anything to win. Our decisions must thoughtfully evaluate the *right* thing to do under the given circumstances. We may have difficulty expressing what our values are, but they are reflected in everything we do—the way we live, work, and play, and in the goals we set and the way we relate to others. Our values enter into our decision-making process whether we think about it or not.

When José Cardenas of San Antonio, Texas, quit his important job as superintendent of schools, his decision made a very powerful statement of his values. He quit because he felt that the decisions he was forced to make concerning budget expenditures (controlled by state policy) were not in the best interests of the children. After resigning, he organized his own nonprofit organization to serve as an advocate for equity for children, school finance, and the provision of technical support for numerous educational initiatives. José did what he thought was right even though it affected his income, his status in the community, and his future as an educator. The rights of the children were of greatest value to him. When he made the decision to quit, he most probably didn't ask himself what his values were, but they are obviously reflected in the decision and his actions.

Leadership demands the skill of open, prompt, and caring decision making. Decision making—like developing a shared vision, opening our minds and hearts to different points of view, and active listening—takes practice. We become better decision makers by making more decisions. Decision making at its best is a challenge, so we frequently find ourselves procrastinating—delaying a decision because we fear the risk. Almost all decisions involve some level of risk. In the next chapter we will discuss risk taking as another essential element of effective leadership.

Chapter Nine

He Who Hesitates Is Lost!

*Dead-end professionals are generally those who have
learned that doing what you are told ensures longevity
and that taking risks is risky business.*
—BETTY FRIEDAN

The issue of risk taking is a paradox that most of us face at some
point in both our personal and professional lives. We are always in
search of change or looking for something original, yet we can be
deeply uncomfortable with taking a risk or trying something different. As John Gardner tells us, "One of the reasons mature people stop learning is that they become less and less willing to risk
failure."[1] Risk taking is an indispensable part of leadership. When
we look around us for creative people who are making a difference, we quickly recognize that they are the risk takers. They have
the courage to try new ways, even when the going looks tough and
they are not sure of the outcome. Individuals who have the potential for leadership are willing to take risks because they know that
being overcautious and indecisive kills opportunity. Non–risk takers are hesitant, waiting for a better time, a less risky situation, or
assured results.

An example of extraordinary risk taking is reflected in the development of the Dash-80 airplane on which many of us have been
passengers. When Boeing was developing the Dash-80 as the airplane of the future, the company was having many serious problems. The CEO was very worried that a $16 million investment was

going to be a complete loss. However, a test pilot by the name of Tex disagreed with him. He was confident that the difficulties could be handled and that the plane would be in high demand by the Aircraft Industries Association (AIA).

Problems plagued every step of the testing process for this plane. Every test flight seemed to be burdened with another disaster. A smashed nose gear, inadequate landing wheels, and insufficient lift were just a few of the problems that the company was trying to address.

At one point, the AIA and representatives of the International Air Transport Association were holding a joint meeting in Seattle. The Gold Cup hydroplane races were being held at the same time. The CEO of Boeing invited the industry dignitaries to watch the events from three yachts he had chartered for the occasion. As a special treat, he also told Tex to stage a simple flyby of the Dash-80 so that everyone could see the airplane of the future. He knew that the industry was waiting for this prototype and that many were beginning to believe it was taking too long to develop.

Tex never did anything halfway. He knew the CEO was worried about the stability of the plane, but he felt confident that the problems had been finally addressed and that he could wow the audience by rolling the plane with complete success. He had secretly and successfully tried it during a test run. He loved the plane and wanted to show what it could really do. Contrary to his orders to *stage a simple flyby,* he completed a 360-degree barrel roll in full view of 300,000 awed spectators! This impressed the industry officials, but the CEO, who almost had a heart attack when he saw what Tex was doing, was very unhappy and angry. In his eyes the risk had been enormous! To Tex—who had secretly tried it before—it was the thing to do to sell the plane.

The story goes that the CEO didn't fire Tex for his incredible risk, but it took him more than twenty years to forgive him![2] This act might be considered the extreme of risk taking; not only did Tex take a risk that might have cost his life, but he also acted against the will of his boss. His experience as a test pilot and previous experience rolling this plane told him that he could take the risk. He also had enough confidence and trust in the reaction of the CEO to risk a long-standing relationship with him and with the company.

Exhibit 9.1. Personal Risk Index.

1. Taking management risks makes good sense only if there are no acceptable alternatives.   agree   disagree

2. I generally prefer stimulation over security.   agree   disagree

3. I have confidence in my ability to recover from my mistakes, no matter how big.   agree   disagree

4. I would promote someone with unlimited potential but limited experience to a key position over someone with limited potential but more experience.   agree   disagree

5. Anything worth doing is worth doing less than perfectly.   agree   disagree

6. I believe opportunity generally knocks only once.   agree   disagree

7. It is better to ask for permission than to beg for forgiveness.   agree   disagree

8. Success in management is as much a matter of luck as ability.   agree   disagree

9. Given a choice, I would choose a $3,000 annual raise over a $10,000 bonus that I had about a one-in-three chance of winning.   agree   disagree

10. I can handle big losses and disappointments with little difficulty.   agree   disagree

11. If forced to choose between them, I would choose safety over achievement.   agree   disagree

12. Failure is the long way to management success.   agree   disagree

13. I tolerate ambiguity and unpredictability well.   agree   disagree

14. I would rather feel intense disappointment than intense regret.   agree   disagree

15. When making a decision with uncertain consequences, my potential losses are my greatest concern.   agree   disagree

Scoring:
Give yourself one point for each of the following statements with which you agree: 2, 3, 4, 5, 10, 13, 14. Give yourself one point for each of the following statements with which you disagree: 1, 6, 7, 8, 9, 11, 12, 15.

Calculate your total. A score of 11 or higher indicates strong pro-risk attitudes; 6–10, medium-strong pro-risk attitudes; and 5 or below, weak pro-risk attitudes.

My score _____

Source: Calvert, G. *High-Wire Management: Risk-Taking Tactics for Leaders, Innovators, and Trailblazers.* San Francisco: Jossey-Bass, 1993, pp. 43–44. Reprinted (with minor changes) with permission from the publisher.

Are You a Risk Taker?

Do you try to stretch and put yourself in new and different situations? Does the possibility of a risk make you nervous? Take a few minutes to complete the exercise in Exhibit 9.1 to assess your comfort level with risk taking. It is purely nonscientific; think of it as a fun tool to help you get to know yourself better.

Then assess your need to feel in control when taking risks by selecting one of the choices from each of the following pairs on page 110, Exhibit 9.2.

These two exercises are just another means to help you understand how you view the world, to help you understand yourself better. There isn't any perfect tool to determine your readiness for risk taking, so just have fun working with these.

What is your conclusion—are you a risk taker? If you are, keep strengthening that skill and help others gain the confidence to move in creative directions as well. If the results indicate that you shy away from taking risks, then take some time to reflect on why this is the case. Then use this knowledge to help you develop a plan for your own personal growth and development as a risk taker.

Risk Taking and Courage

Charles Kettering of General Motors points out the value of being willing to fail—and learn from it.

> An inventor is simply a person who doesn't take his education too seriously. From the time a person is six years old until he graduates

Exhibit 9.2. Control Index.

_____ Hard work and determination lead to promotions.

_____ Successful people are usually just in the right place at the right time.

_____ The high divorce rate confirms that married people don't try hard enough to get along.

_____ Good marriages result from luck, not effort.

_____ Your financial security depends on your ability.

_____ Luck, not effort, tends to determine who gets promoted.

_____ People are easy to lead if you know how to handle them.

_____ I have little effect on how people behave.

_____ The grades I earned in school came from hard work.

_____ I don't believe I had much influence over the grades I earned in school.

_____ I can change the direction of society if I assert myself.

_____ No one can really affect where this society is heading.

_____ I can control my fate.

_____ Much of what will happen to me is in the hands of fate.

_____ Working harmoniously with others is a skill that can be taught.

_____ Some people can't be satisfied no matter how hard you try.

Which column has the greatest number of checks? If you chose more items in the left column, you are a natural-born risk taker because you believe that you can control events. If you find that you have checked more items in the right column, you prefer not to take risks.

Source: Calvert, G. _High-Wire Management: Risk-Taking Tactics for Leaders, Innovators, and Trailblazers._ San Francisco: Jossey-Bass, 1993, p. 47. Based on the work of J. Rotter.

from college, he has to take three or four examinations a year. If he flunks once, he is out. But an inventor is almost always failing. He tries and fails maybe a thousand times. If he succeeds once, then he's in. These two things are diametrically opposite. We often say that the biggest job we have is to teach a newly hired employee how to fail intelligently. We have to train him to experiment over and over and to keep on trying and failing until he learns what will work.[3]

Risk taking is definitely something that can be learned, but you don't need to take classes at a nearby university or intensive training programs. In fact, the process is quite simple. *Try new things. Be creative.* Place yourself in situations that are slightly uncomfortable—stretch! Even if you fail, you will learn more about how something can or can't be done—and you'll learn more about your willingness and ability to make decisions and to take risks. Others—your boss, supervisor, or colleagues—may also recognize that you are willing to stretch and offer you opportunities over and beyond your normal duties. As Sheila Bethel says, "Unlike rubber bands, we humans become stronger through constant stretching. If we stretch a rubber band too far, it will either break or weaken and lose its elasticity. When *we* stretch beyond what may seem to be our limits—when we take daring risks—we may not succeed, but we become stronger. We never go back to the same shape we were in previously."[4]

One can find many examples of successful risk taking or the significance of failures to take a risk. One of my favorites that exemplifies the latter is a wonderful story in Erik Olesen's *Twelve Steps to Mastering the Winds of Change.* He describes an incident that took place when Calvin Coolidge was president. Coolidge apparently invited a group of friends from his hometown to dine with him at the White House. Unaccustomed to the sophistication of the White House, the guests were worried about their table manners, so they decided to do everything exactly as Coolidge did. This strategy succeeded, until coffee was served. The president poured his coffee into his saucer. The guests were surprised and hesitant, but then they too did the same. Coolidge then added sugar and cream. His guests did, too. What surprise and chagrin they must have felt when Coolidge then bent over and put his saucer on the floor for the cat![5]

This is a crystal-clear example of what can happen if we lack self-confidence, lack the courage to be ourselves and to do what we believe is right, lack the courage to make a decision that might not be in agreement with those around us. Being different is always a risk, but following the crowd at best preserves the status quo—and can lead to something as ridiculous as feeding your coffee to the cat.

Leaders are courageous people. They don't waste much time worrying about what other people might think of them; they are more concerned about doing what is right and effective. They make every attempt to weave a shared vision, to align others toward a goal, and then with enthusiasm, energy, and commitment they are willing to walk near the edge and even do things that raise the eyebrows of those around them if needed to achieve the goal—to get the job done!

Many of us are too concerned about what other people think of us. We plan our lives and daily actions to fit the expectations of those around us. We plan to do only what we are absolutely certain will not ruffle any feathers. We carefully screen out any ideas that might cause us to make a mistake. In so doing, we stifle our creativity and self-confidence, make change very difficult to handle, avoid all risk taking, and create a controlled, predictable, uninspired environment. Yes, we dig ourselves into a rut of sameness! Do you remember *The Wizard of Oz*? Can you recall the character of the cowardly lion? Even the cowardly lion realized that being a safe plodder was not the way to succeed in life. Those driven by insecurity creep gingerly through life, hoping to make it safely to the next toehold. *Every move is so carefully and cautiously planned to avoid failure at any cost that by the time the decision is made, the opportunity is lost.*

One of my friends speaks about the 60 percent rule for taking action. If you have 60 percent of the information needed to take action, *take it*—don't wait, hoping that somehow you'll be able to get 100 percent of the facts you need. The 100 percent may never come, and then the opportunity to be creative, to make a difference, will be lost. I am not suggesting that we act irresponsibly or ignore the concerns of people around us. It is important to get along with our colleagues and neighbors, but we must also be willing to take risks and accept the responsibility for our decisions. If we have listened carefully to what everyone involved has to say, if we have weighed all the alternatives, then the next step is to take the risk, make a decision, and act. Waiting for 100 percent agreement or information on anything is the surest way to make no decision at all. Remember what we discussed in the last chapter. There are times for consensus in decision making, but there are also times when you and you alone must take the risk and make the decision.

Let me continue the story of a remarkable pair of citizen leaders I met a few years ago. One is a Catholic priest, Father Bill Cunningham, and the other a housewife, Eleanor Josaitis, both of Detroit. I talked about Eleanor and Father Bill in the last chapter. When the city of Detroit was being torn apart by riots, racism, and hate, and most people were moving out of the city and into the suburbs as fast as they could, Eleanor decided to leave her comfortable home in the suburbs and move into the city with her husband and children. Father Bill also chose to stay at his parish in the inner city, rather than accept a comfortable position in a safe suburb. Both these individuals lost many friends because of their decision; even close family members ridiculed them and refused to visit or acknowledge them as part of the family. But Eleanor and Father Bill knew that they had to live their faith and beliefs, and be a part of the solution to problems of racial inequity. Their decision clearly reflected their core set of values.

These two people not only moved into the inner city, they also became citizen activists. Father Bill, Eleanor, and a small group of friends and believers organized and trained more than fifty clergymen in an attempt to help them confront the problems of hate, fear, and racism in their parishes. When the situation was at its worst and there was once again fear of what they called "hot summers," with threats of fire, property damage, and murder, these two citizen leaders decided that one way to put up a barrier to the riots was to throw a huge street party. What a risk! The mayor, the bishop, the police department, everyone in positions of power and importance fought the idea. Even their closest friends told them that they were crazy. The city council president told them, "If you bring a crowd downtown, you'll blow this city away!"

Father Bill and Eleanor prayed and decided that they had to take the risk. They organized hundreds of volunteers of every color and creed. They worked hard to involve everyone, even the Black Panthers. After weeks of exhausting work, their dream of a carnival in the streets where blacks, whites, and browns had *fun* together—rather than fights—materialized. No major negative incident occurred. The event was so successful that the street carnival became a tradition and received strong support from the city leaders in subsequent years.

This was obviously a very risky thing to do; it could have back-fired and caused terrible devastation. These two individuals took the risk, but they didn't do it alone. It was a calculated risk—they knew the many resources they would need for this idea to be successful. They also had a deep sense of faith and spirituality that gave them the strength and courage to stand by their convictions. They called upon hundreds of like-minded individuals from every walk of life, and spent many hours persuading those who might have been counted among the angry, hostile group to share in their vision of a peaceful city. They also clearly exhibited the seamless nature of leadership and followership in all their activities.

Effective leaders in any organization or community are risk takers. They can sometimes be described as unconventional with a nagging need to try something new—to create. In fact, there are times when they may be considered insubordinate or mischievous because they get bored easily and would rather ask forgiveness than ask permission! These are motivators, they inspire people to perform, and they energize people by their occasional surprise action. This is not to be misunderstood as advocating behavior that can be termed acting like a loose cannon or a bull in a china shop, but rather creative risk taking reinforced by sound judgment, common sense, and personal responsibility. The Boeing test pilot decided to ask forgiveness rather than permission, but his in-depth knowledge of the plane, his flying experience, and his intuitive sense of "this is the time" led to success. Father Bill and Eleanor convinced many others to take the risk and share their vision of peace and nonviolence. The success of their efforts can be seen at the FOCUS: HOPE organization they initiated. Their many achievements are indicative of creative risk taking.

Taking Risks and Making Mistakes

Risk is inherent in almost every successful innovation. Leaders put themselves and others at risk whenever they decide to plunge into a venture that has not been tried before. But if we want to promote efforts to improve the way things are done, then we must lead in taking risks. Of course, whenever I encourage people to take risks, I am challenged by the question, "How can anyone judge whether a risk is foolhardy or reasonable?" Only you can answer that question. Each of us must determine our own level of comfort with trying something new, with the level of the stretch. Frequently our risk level can be measured by our willingness to accept and admit failure or mistakes and by the willingness of our organization to encourage and allow mistakes.

There is no simple test to protect yourself from serious mistakes; one person's risk is another's normal activity. Knowing yourself, your organization, or your community is an important factor in arriving at a decision to take a risk. I can recall interviewing a young candidate for a fellowship program. One of the interview questions addressed to each candidate involved his or her attitude toward risk taking. This young woman was asked what she considered to be the greatest risk she had ever taken. Her response surprised some of the interviewers. She didn't talk about mountain climbing or bungee jumping! She described taking a trip through Europe, alone and unplanned, as her greatest risk. Some of the well-traveled interviewers had difficulty accepting this as a risk. In their minds it was a conservative, everyday occurrence. However, for this sheltered young woman, the trip alone to unknown countries was a stretch. What she didn't tell us—but we discovered later—was that she had absolutely no fear of the very physically demanding and risky sport of mountain climbing.

The people who had interviewed her were petrified at the thought of this activity. For them, travel through Europe was simple and easy; mountain climbing was risk taking. For her, the exact opposite was true. This is a clear example of how important it is for each of us to come to terms with our own reality, skill, and level of comfort when determining risk. We all know people who will take daring physical risks but are terrified of speaking in public, while some well-known teachers or public speakers would never set foot on a river raft or attempt to climb a mountain.

Experience: An Excellent Teacher

Inevitably, discussions of risk taking lead to discussions about a fear of failure. One person who has overcome amazing obstacles said:

> To be an effective leader, you not only have to get the group of followers on the right path, but you must be able to convince them that whatever obstacle stands in the way ahead, whether it's a tree or a building that blocks the view, you're going to get around it.

You're not going to be put off by the apparent barriers to your goal. All journeys are filled with potholes and mines, but the only way we can move beyond them is to approach them, and recognize them for what they are. You have to see that it's only a tree, or a stone, or a mountain, and it's not insurmountable. Everywhere you trip is where the treasure lies.[6]

Experience is a master teacher. All of us learn by doing, and so if you do anything at all you are bound to make some mistakes. The trick is to learn from them—to be creative—to not stumble over the same tree branch or obstacle twice. Think of every mistake as another valuable learning experience. Believe me, much of what we can learn by our mistakes can never be taught in the classroom. Thomas Edison developed thousands of filaments that didn't work before he discovered the correct one for the incandescent lamp. Abraham Lincoln lost more than a dozen elections before he finally got voted into office. Leaders do not view mistakes as failures, but rather as opportunities to learn something new.

Whether you are thinking about leadership in terms of your community or family, or if you are striving for upward mobility in your place of employment, learning through experience and risk taking are key factors in achieving your goals.

As noted in *The Lessons of Experience,* "In a survey of more than seven hundred chief executives, conducted by Charles Margerison and Andrew Kakabadse for the American Management Association, 'early leadership experience' received a high ranking among the key influences on their career development. According to these CEOs, leadership is a practical skill that can be learned only through actual experience, preferably before the age of thirty."[7] Experience, trying something new, stretching, are important factors to be considered in the education of our young people.

The idea of leadership education reflects the work of many researchers who have found that much of what is taught in our colleges and universities is excellent theory, but practical applications are completely lacking. Therefore, young would-be managers are totally unprepared for the realities of managing, and young potential leaders can only learn to lead by leading. You have to be willing to take calculated risks, to learn by your mistakes. You don't need a college education to learn to take a risk, to make decisions, to be open-minded. It simply takes practice. You can earn an A in a class on decision making, but until you are put to the test and confronted with some serious decisions, some calculated risks, your skill and insight will remain untested.

The basic task of creative leadership is to set a future direction. As I have said earlier, it recognizes the dynamic tension between "what is" and "what could be" and encourages calculated risk taking to produce change that will carry us toward the "what could be." That is a primary function.

Organizational Culture and Risk Taking

Not all organizations have a culture that encourages risk taking. Some organizations that are models of fairness on the reward side of the equation are often found to be rather rigid when it comes to mistakes or failures. In these organizations, you will find many stories about whom to avoid and what not to say or do. In fact, you will find that in some organizations the employees firmly believe in the premise: "One mistake and you're out." This is very unfortunate, and such an organization will probably become a has-been much faster than anyone there anticipates. The inability of these organizations to foster the development of young, talented leadership leads to their eventual demise.

The most successful organizations are those that have room for individuals who are always a little different. These iconoclasts continually prod and push us to see new ways of doing things, new approaches to old problems. They challenge our comfort levels and sometimes they even prove to be somewhat irritating. Communities and organizations that accept and nurture such creativity and risk taking are most successful at establishing a culture of openness and futuristic thinking.

All individuals have something to contribute to the improvement of their organization, their society, their family, or their community. There may be times when you will be called upon to lead, and other times when it will be your responsibility to organize, manage, and follow. However, it is always our responsibility to know ourselves, to develop the self-confidence to take calculated risks, and to act on this knowledge with courage and commitment. *We need to be willing to take the risk of pouring our coffee into our cup even when everyone else is pouring it into the saucer!*

Chapter Ten

Understanding Power and Love

There is nothing noble about being superior to others. True nobility is being superior to your previous self.
—UNKNOWN

You will recall that in the first few chapters I stressed that we must not confuse leadership with status, position, or title. Similarly, leadership and power are not synonymous. According to John Gardner, who served six different U.S. presidents in a variety of leadership capacities, "We must not confuse leadership with power. Leaders always have some measure of power, rooted in their capacity to persuade, but many people with power are without leadership gifts. Their power derives from money, or from the capacity to inflict harm, or from control of some piece of institutional machinery, or from access to the media. A military dictator has power. The thug who sticks a gun in your ribs has power. Leadership is something else."[1]

As the world becomes more interdependent, it is imperative that we expand our ideas of what power and leadership mean and how they are acted out. We need to learn to grow beyond our own egos, and recognize that leadership without power is no leadership at all; but power without caring, commitment, and empathy can become a selfish tyranny. Our effectiveness as leaders is in direct proportion to our effectiveness as human beings.

Leadership and power are not the same thing. They intersect at many points, but it is important to understand the differences.

A construction foreman, a CEO of a corporation, or a tax assessor may have the power to control certain outcomes and yet have absolutely no leadership abilities. We have all met extraordinarily bright individuals who have such poor relational skills and bad judgment that we would hesitate to follow any direction from them. These individuals may have power without leadership ability. On the other hand, there are individuals with excellent leadership ability who do not have titles or positions that automatically give them power. In order to effect the vision they propose, they develop a base of power through their communication skills, integrity, or ability to work with people.

Think of Martin Luther King Jr., Maggie Kuhn (the organizer of the Grey Panthers), Eleanor Josaitis from Detroit, or Sarah, the teenager from New England. All these individuals developed a base of power that evolved from their heart and leadership capabilities, not from a title or position. This is not to say that power that evolves from title, position, money, or intelligence is necessarily bad. I am merely stressing my firm belief that *no one is powerless*. We can build our bases of power on our inner strength, love, and respect for others.

It is our responsibility to understand the accountability that comes with power. So let's reflect on where power fits in our growing chain of leadership knowledge and skills. Without trust and integrity, an action-oriented and dynamic environment is nothing but a pipe dream. It takes an environment of trust and integrity to support a variety of decision-making styles. Without a willingness to take a risk, we may find ourselves lacking the passion or power to move to another level of accomplishment. Without the skills of positive listening and communicating with meaning, our vision will be narrow and lack the insight of others. And weaving a shared vision can only be accomplished if we respect and value the different needs and dreams of those who surround us.

All these factors are links in the chain that make up the essence of leadership. We have spent the last several chapters discussing these links and sharing the lives of people who have reflected success and failure in dealing with them. Now we need to spend some time reflecting on another link, *real power*—power that emanates from our growing ability to understand and love ourselves and those around us.

Powerful Versus Powerless

Understanding and developing these links in the chain will lead us to an understanding of power as the actual expenditure of personal energy to achieve one's passion or mission in life. It can be considered as the source of energy that helps us find our voice and work collaboratively with others. According to Stephen Covey, *"Power* is the faculty or capacity to act, the strength and potency to accomplish something. It is the vital energy to make choices and decisions. It also includes the capacity to overcome deeply embedded habits and to cultivate higher, more effective ones."[2]

In this chapter, I focus on shared power rather than on the power that emanates from title, position, or money. I am doing so because I firmly believe that fast-paced change and readily available information are slowly but surely displacing the old hierarchical forms of power and authority. Recently, I found this pointed doggerel in a book by Allan Cox, *Straight Talk for Monday Morning:*

> Oh where, oh where
> has authority gone?
> Oh where, oh where can it be?
> It's all drained out of the boss's big stick
> 'Tis a network of thee, me, and we.[3]

According to Cox, this does not mean that your boss has no authority (power) over you, but rather that the increase of readily available information is moving us to new systems of power and learning that are much more dispersed.

So many of the people I meet every day consider themselves powerless, or believe that being powerful means having authority over people. Having power over people cannot be categorized as a great leadership accomplishment. In fact, people who have the power that comes with title or authority are sometimes the major contributors toward a feeling of powerlessness in others. College professors, secretaries, children, teachers, taxpayers, minorities, handicapped individuals, almost anyone you can think of might tell you that they feel powerless in their positions because of an authority figure in their lives. Are they really powerless?

Sometimes when I hear people use the word *powerless* I question their meaning. Perhaps they are merely referring to the natural give and take that we can expect to find in every aspect of our lives. In some respects it is comparable to the concept of leadership and followership, which are the two sides of one sheet of paper. However, whole portions of our society feel they are permanently powerless as victims of a powerful system. Notice the disgracefully low voter turnout in cities and townships across the country. Could this be due to the feeling among large populations of people that they have no power to change the status quo? Could this be a reflection of the growing belief that others have power over us?

The first step to overcoming the feeling of powerlessness is the will to change. The second is learning about ourselves, our relationship with others, and what we need to do to build coalitions of like-minded people. Power is first of all about self-control—it is about being in charge of the direction our lives are taking. It is about making choices. Then, when we understand ourselves and our passion, it is important to understand the balance of *external power* for action and *internal power* for reflection and compassion for others.

I recall learning a valuable lesson about the power of self-control, building coalitions, and not overreacting in disagreeable situations from a venerable African American gentleman. Stephen Wright has served as president of more than one institution of higher education. He has been a leader nationally and internationally for youth and for equal rights. He is a man of prestige and wisdom who, although retired, has continued to serve young people in a variety of capacities.

On one occasion, I had invited him to share his perspective of the benefits of a fellowship program with the board of trustees of the W.K. Kellogg Foundation. One of the board members persisted in a line of questioning that I perceived as a somewhat narrow view of evaluation. After we left the meeting, I began to fret and fuss about this board member's narrow focus, while I completely ignored the positive feedback from the other members of the board. Stephen quietly listened to my frustration and then said, "Larraine, you don't use a cannon to kill a gnat." I was silenced! In one short sentence, he taught me volumes. I realized I was overreacting to the power and prestige of the board member. I had lost sight of the strength of the positive feedback by the other eight board members and had chosen to behave like a powerless victim. It was a lesson I will never forget.

Another powerful story is that of Kennet, a young college student. It is an interesting insight into one person's development from a sense of powerlessness to one of power. Kennet was born in Puerto Rico and moved to the United States with his parents when he was in the second grade. He had already learned to read, write, and speak Spanish. He joined a second-grade class where only English was spoken, which quickly put him behind his classmates. He was frustrated in attempting to learn with the others; he felt excluded and eventually his frustration led to anger and rebellion. His youth, language problems, and lack of understanding by teachers led him to believe that he was powerless in the situation. He felt that authority figures had power over his life and he was destined to survive according to their rules and measures. He began to act out his frustration. He learned to live down to everyone's expectations of him, and was finally expelled from the private school he was attending. The future did not look very bright for Kennet.

Up to this point, teachers were negative about Kennet and judged that he simply wasn't capable of academic achievement. Fortunately, when Kennet entered a large public high school, his reputation as a low achiever did not follow him. He got a fresh start. His first semester, he startled his family and himself by earning all A's and B's. At the same time, one of his teachers suggested that he become involved with a youth leadership program sponsored by the Urban League. The director of this program took a special interest in Kennet and, through her caring intervention, his self-confidence was gradually restored. This was the beginning of a whole new life for him!

By the end of his sophomore year, Kennet was involved in every opportunity presented to him. The teachers saw in him the energy and enthusiasm to become a powerful influence in the school and community. They created opportunities for him to use his leadership skills not only within his school, but across the entire district by representing his school at sessions with elected and appointed officials. His world had become a much bigger, better place. His willingness to change had taken him from powerless to powerful!

Kennet is now at the University of Michigan. He has found that he has the potential to become a fine young leader. Now his life goal is to work with young people of color as a teacher. He says, "I want to help [kids] realize that they have the power to change the world. They don't have to be passive." He would like to be an active participant, either as leader or follower, in the reform of the public education system so that children of all backgrounds can have the opportunity to achieve their potential.

Although Kennet is young, he already understands the effective use of both power and love as tools in the process of helping people take charge of their lives and their communities. His story clearly portrays that the first step to overcoming powerlessness is the will to stay open to change.

Perceptions of Power

In many organizations, people see power as finite.[4] It is something they strategize to possess and then guard as a valuable personal possession. From their perspective, power is something only a few can have; it is very dependent on title, position, and personal connections. Therefore, once you have it, you must guard it tenaciously! In their view, power is comparable to savings in the bank. If a person has $5 million and someone else takes $2 million, then there is only $3 million left. Something is lost—power has been taken away. From this perspective, everything comes in only limited amounts— whether it be dollars or power—and in order to pass it around, it must be taken away from one and given to another.[5] Where people have this perception of power, there will always be intrigue, lack of trust, jealousy, deception, rivalry for position, and autocratic leadership.

There is no shared vision in such an environment, and loyal, supportive followership is viewed as a weakness or failure. Individuals caught in these circumstances exhibit passivity, cynicism, and lack of commitment. Creativity lies dormant while the people wait for the authority figure to tell them what to do. This in turn invites abuse of power. What a vicious circle!

If, however, the general conception of power is that it becomes more valuable and powerful as it is shared, we observe a very different environment. We will find a trusting, enthusiastic atmosphere in the workplace, and creativity and productivity will be apparent. In this view, power can be compared to a candle. Just suppose that we are all in a very dark, cold room. We all have candles but you are the only person with a candle that is burning. There are no other sources of flame or matches available. You alone have in your possession light, heat, and energy. *You have power.* You can either clutch it to yourself, or you can share it. If you share the flame with those around you, what will happen? Will you lose anything? On the contrary, all of us, including you, will gain because of the increased light, heat, and energy generated by multiple candles.

Empowering others is a way to increase the total potential of power. In situations where this concept is understood and practiced, no one loses—everyone gains. Sharing power, empowerment, or enabling people means removing the barriers of position, title, or rank that box people in and inhibit them from performing at their peak efficiency. It means providing them with whatever is necessary to develop a sense of confidence and ownership over parts of the process in which they are involved, and it requires that they accept a share of the responsibility for the entire endeavor.

This latter perception of power is found in individuals who understand risk taking, weaving a shared vision, openness to many perspectives and the essential nature of spirituality in the life of a leader. Such a leader knows that whether it is power or simply caring or kindness that is given away, it usually comes back full circle. It may not come back in the same form that it was given; but the satisfaction of receiving appreciation, experiencing creative new ideas from others, observing enthusiasm as hard work is performed, or accepting the warmth of true friendship leads to new levels of personal growth and organizational harmony. Power and love may appear to be a paradox, but they are, indeed, a new-age duet!

Pluses and Minuses of Shared Power

When a leader shares power with others and encourages them to develop their own potential, that leader is creating something that will survive long after he or she has moved to another role. This is in striking contrast to those situations where we may find a charismatic leader who loves the status of a position, and who is unwilling to share the power and perceived glory. Status-bound leaders tend to create dependency in those who work with them. When they move on, they leave behind a weakened environment and weakened people who cannot carry on the work that the powerful leader orchestrated. On the other hand, leaders who understand shared power can be assured of creating a legacy that has the potential to continue long after they are gone.

As a member of a nonprofit board, I had the good fortune to observe a leader who understood leadership as service and was very willing to honestly share power. Eileen (not her real name) became the director of a floundering organization dedicated to helping battered women. The organization had been through a troublesome few years and was faced with financial difficulties, staff discontent, and board disagreement. Eileen accepted the position fully aware of the many challenges it would present. She believed that the organization was critically needed in the community. She dedicated herself to making it strong once again. She listened and learned a great deal by spending time with the board members who were unhappy with the direction of the organization. Quietly but effectively, Eileen began an organizational image-building campaign in the community. She recognized the talented members of her staff and included them in the process of weaving a vision for the future of the organization. She delegated responsibility to the bright and competent people she was able to hire, and encouraged them to challenge her. Eileen looked for new board members who would represent a broader cross section of the community, and who could bring her fresh views and more educated opinions.

Eileen is honest, hardworking, and intelligent; she loves people and is willing to assume responsibility. She exudes quiet confidence and is not threatened by sharing power with other competent people on the staff and board. Of course, the sense of self-confidence and security people feel in her presence make her a very powerful person. Eileen's power only partially evolves from her position as director of the shelter for battered women. Her true power is derived from her inner strength and ability to genuinely share power and love with those around her.

Unfortunately, the practice of shared power isn't always carried out with the best of intentions. There can also be a negative rationale for the idea of sharing power. The idea of empowerment is sometimes used as a panacea for all organizational problems. It is seen as a magical solution to problems that really originate from a much deeper conflict—a failure to respect the intellect and creativity of every person within the organization. In some organizations, the changes involving shared power or empowerment may be merely an attempt to shift blame and responsibility for organizational problems from the top management to persons lower on the totem pole. By making it appear that power has been shared, the responsibility for mistakes in judgment can be placed squarely on the shoulders of some unsuspecting person.[6]

If an atmosphere of trust and love is lacking, introducing ideas of shared power can create all sorts of suspicions. The idea may be viewed skeptically by others as an attempt to co-opt people. They may suspect that by creating the illusion that there is a decrease in top-down control and an increase in shared power, an attempt is being made to make them believe that they also have equal participation in decision-making processes. This may be far from the truth.[7] Yes, even the very best ideas can be distorted into negatives.

If we find ourselves caught in a comparable situation, it is our responsibility to act with integrity and courage. It may mean reinforcing strong team coalitions to protect each other. It may require pointing out the actual course of decision making. Or it may mean assuming the role of loyal follower and helping to build a trusting environment. Each situation may require a different approach to achieve trust or equity or justice. However, the characters of true leaders will be reflected in their willingness to assume power for their own position within the community or organization. This is an important step in making change happen.

In *The 21st Century Organization*, Warren Bennis and Michael Mische use a very powerful quote about the character of a true leader: "The leader's character is made up of a tripod of forces: ambition and drive; competence and expertise; integrity and moral fabric. All three are needed, and all three have to be in balance, or the tripod topples. Get a leader with only drive but not competence and integrity, and you get a demagogue. Get someone with competence but absent integrity and drive, and you get a technocrat. Get seduced by someone who has ambition and competence but lacks integrity, and you get a destructive achiever."[8]

Power that comes only from a title, position, or box on an organizational chart is very fleeting power. When the title is gone, the power is gone. True power—internal power—the power that emanates from within a person moves with the person, regardless of title or position. It is a sign of integrity and moral strength.

Wise Use of Power

As you can see, the sources of power are many and varied. Some of these sources easily lead us to the idea of sharing and compassion that will be essential in the coming century. Others simply cause us to cling to the status quo reflected in the power of position or title. Money and possessions, property, position, personal attractiveness, expertise, intelligence, charisma, the capacity to motivate others, all these and a long list of other sources of power come into play in any normal day of community or organizational living. Tough-minded, strong but caring, compassionate leaders use power wisely and with restraint, regardless of its source.

The discreet use of power takes wisdom, tough-mindedness, and good judgment. Joe Batten, in *Tough-Minded Leadership,* tells us what *tough* really means. He says, "If I place two pieces of material the same size, shape and form on an anvil, and one is made of granite, the other of leather, and then hit each with a hammer, what will happen? The granite will shatter into pieces, precisely *because* it is hard. . . . The leather is barely dented, precisely because it is *not* hard. It is flexible, malleable, resilient, elastic, durable, supple—and it is *tough!*"[9]

Likewise, Lao-tzu wrote in 600 B.C., "Water is fluid, soft, and yielding. But water will wear away rock, which is rigid and cannot yield. As a rule, whatever is fluid, soft, and yielding will overcome whatever is rigid and hard. . . . This is another paradox: what is soft is strong."[10]

Without good judgment, compassion, and wisdom in the use of power, little of lasting value will be achieved. With the proper use of power one can accomplish a great deal. To lead wisely, one needs to be strong but gentle—strong as leather or water to tackle the tough issues, and gentle, supple, and fluid enough to keep the solutions humane. One needs to be tough enough to challenge others, flexible and self-confident enough to share power, demanding enough not to settle for easy answers, and patient enough to know that good things happen in due time—perhaps more time than is usually anticipated.

Power, well used, has tremendous binding capabilities. It holds all the other essential qualities of leadership together. It energizes people and, sometimes in miraculous ways, uncovers necessary resources. When you use power wisely and gently you show those you are working with that you can be trusted, that you are willing to share the power and that you will not take advantage of them. Trust is the bedrock of achievement and excellence in families, communities, and organizations.

Stages of Power

One of the best books I have ever read concerning the topic of power is Janet Hagberg's *Real Power: Stages of Personal Power in Organizations.* Janet talks about six stages of personal power. Let's look at a few of them, listed in Figure 10.1.

Stage One is the behavior that evolves when a person believes that he or she is powerless. Insecurity and fear lead to coercive action. Hagberg's research leads her to the conclusion that people

Figure 10.1. Hagberg's Model of Leadership and Power.

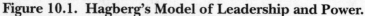

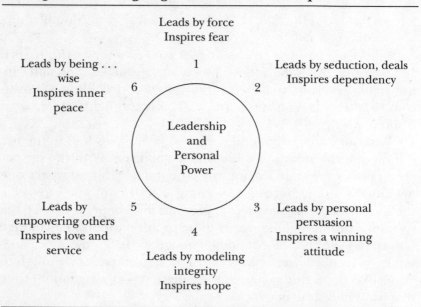

Leads by force
Inspires fear

Leads by being . . .
wise
Inspires inner
peace

1

6   2

Leads by seduction, deals
Inspires dependency

Leadership
and
Personal
Power

Leads by
empowering others
Inspires love and
service

5   3

4

Leads by personal
persuasion
Inspires a winning
attitude

Leads by modeling
integrity
Inspires hope

Source: Hagberg, J. O. *Real Power: Stages of Personal Power in Organizations.* (rev. ed.) Salem, Wis.: Sheffield, 1994, p. 157. Reprinted with permission of the publisher.

with power that evolves from titles or positions are sometimes at Stage Two, but predominantly at Stage Three. She asserts that the latter is the most prominent form of leadership power found in organizations. "Prime examples of Stage Three leadership are corporate or organizational ladder-climbing people. To get to the top of a Stage Three organization one must learn to be a Stage Three leader par excellence. So one mimics the behavior of all the leaders who are farther along, hoping to inherit their formula for success." [11]

Study the diagram for a few minutes. Where would you classify yourself on this leadership and power cycle right now? Your organization? What kind of leader do you hope to become? What kind of leadership do you believe we need in this changing society? How do we become wise leaders who understand how to use power and love? If you are genuinely interested in the idea of power and love, please refer to books listed in the Resources section.

In an earlier chapter, we talked about future trends and demographic changes facing us in the next century. It will not be enough to hinge our future on leaders who have power derived from symbols—or climbing the ladder of titles. We need leaders who have achieved Stages Four or Five in Janet Hagberg's cycle. The world is at a turning point and we will need wise, inspired, visionary leaders on every level who understand the true meaning of the shared power of a democracy. The basic idea of democracy is that people can and should govern themselves. Everyone has the capacity to participate in the deliberate shaping of their communities and their lives. "The power of democracy lies in transforming people from consumers, victims, and exploiters into responsible citizens." [12]

To develop a leadership style that empowers others, is wise, and inspires inner peace, we need to make that leap in our understanding that sharing power is not losing anything, but rather *gaining* a great deal. We need to reshape our thinking to embrace the new view that leadership and loyal, supportive followership are every person's responsibility. This does not necessarily mean that we will be all powerful, famous, and wealthy, or have a wonderful position or title. It does mean that, like Eileen and Kennet, we should strive to become compassionate, loving, visionary people who care about others—people who are committed to helping others to a higher plane of excellence and leadership—people who understand that spiritual, inner power is just as important as external power.

This entire discussion of shared power and love implies a new way of thinking and an openness to change. Today, the pace of change we face is extremely swift. This causes us great discomfort because the very core of human nature is to resist change. Many organizations that were designed to solve problems are out of touch and have lost their capacity to respond to new, demanding problems. Power is still tightly held in the hands of a few individuals at the top of a hierarchical pyramid, while motivation gradually disappears and values decay. If the forces of renewal and creative thinking and an in-depth understanding of democracy are not incorporated into the fabric of our organizations and communities, the end of a democratic society as we know it may be predictable. In the next chapter, we will discuss change as another link in the chain of the essence of leadership, and as an important factor in our present environment.

Chapter Eleven

Creating the Future

*Of all the creatures of earth, only human beings can
change their patterns. Man alone is the architect of his
destiny. . . . Human beings, by changing the inner
attitudes of their minds, can change the outer aspects
of their lives.*
—WILLIAM JAMES

Creating the future means being one step ahead of the forces of
change and moving in the direction in which our intuition and
intelligence indicate we are already headed. It means keeping our
eyes and ears open to change of all kinds—social, cultural, economic, demographic, government, lifestyle, technological, and
global, and trying to sense the rhythm of these changes. It also
means keeping our sensitivities fine-tuned to the kind of personal
change that may be required by any or all of these trends. This is
only the thinking half of anticipating change. Equally important is
the action half, which means coming up with innovative ideas that
respond to these changes and bring them to life.

Change Happens!

To make things better, to *create the future*, to make a difference; that's
what leadership is all about. Leadership, we have said, requires passion, a deep sense of spirituality, the personal and interpersonal
skills to reach out to people, a vision of "what could be" rather than
a concentration on "what is," and a recognition that all these aspects of leadership require an understanding and acceptance of

change. In previous chapters, we have explored the lives of individuals who have recognized that change and personal growth are essential factors in the process of effective leadership and followership. Now we'll spend a little more time talking about the reality of constant change.

Let me share a business example of what I am talking about. For much of this century, Singer was one of the best-known sewing machine companies in the world. In the late seventies, they began to see a decline in business. At first they attributed the drop in sales to the weather, then they blamed the oil crisis, then they blamed the influx of cheap foreign sewing machines.

Finally the company convened a special task force to study the problem. What they discovered was that the weather, the oil shortage, and the foreign imports had nothing to do with their loss of business. Their business was being affected by "*a lifestyle change:* women entering the work force in record numbers. This new lifestyle changed women's priorities."[1] They had less time and little interest in sewing. Also, there was "a flood of [inexpensive] ready-to-wear clothing from southeast Asian factories and the cost savings of sewing-your-own began to disappear."[2] The leaders of the company had not kept their eyes and ears open for social, economic, and lifestyle changes that might affect their business. Had they been alert, they would have recognized that the growing numbers of women taking jobs outside the home would be a driving force for change into the nineties and far beyond.[3]

Change is inevitable! Yet how many times have we all heard or said, "We've always done it that way," or, "I like it the way it is," or, "The good ol' days were so much better." Well, maybe they were—and maybe they weren't! The real issue here is that perhaps we are not comfortable with change. However, whether we like it or not, all we need to do is reflect on our own lives and environment to recognize that change happens! There will be changes in the environment, changes in our families, changes in our communities, changes in the places we work, and changes within ourselves. The demographics and trends strongly indicate that worldwide change is occurring constantly. How we handle change is an indicator of our leadership capabilities. Leaders anticipate change; they create it rather than waiting for it to engulf them and leave them in a state of turmoil.

Resistance to Change

It is important for us to understand the underlying causes of resistance to change and try to develop a plan by which we can manage and enjoy the inevitable. Recently I read a practical and realistic quote from King Whitney Jr. in a health newsletter: "Change has considerable psychological impact on the human mind. *To the fearful,* change is threatening because it means that things may get worse. *To the hopeful,* change is encouraging because things may get better. *To the confident,* change is inspiring because the challenge exists to make things better."[4]

Leaders do not fear change; they are hopeful and confident, so they look forward to change—it excites them. Leaders foresee change and use it as a stepping-stone, instead of allowing it to be a stumbling block. People who have the courage and passion to assume leadership responsibilities have the confidence to anticipate change, as well as to think through and creatively respond to it.

Things that are familiar to us, that we are comfortable with, are always less threatening than new things. Think what a shock the printing press must have been to the monks and scribes who had created all books by hand-printing them. People either laughed or called the Wright Brothers idiots when they heard that they were going to build a flying machine. Could we have ever dreamed that computers would exist and that they would become small enough to fit into our briefcases or coat pockets? During the scorching summer of 1995, I frequently wondered how the people in the deep South survived before the advent of air-conditioning! All these changes met with some resistance, but now they are accepted as facts of life.

The following vivid example of change was given in a speech by Joseph Hankin, president of Westchester Community College:

> In the tenth century, Abdul Kassem Ismael, the scholarly grand-vizier of Persia, had a library of 117,000 volumes. On his many travels as a warrior and statesman, he never parted with his beloved books. They were carried about by 400 camels trained to walk in alphabetical order!
>
> Today's speech is about the need to change. If we utilized the camel caravan, in order to hold the 6 million books in the

Pals-Waldo consortium collection, we would need more than 20,000; if the WLS libraries were to join in, we would need another 7,000 camels! Imagine all that feed and all that dung! We cannot carry our books about by camel today, but we can by computer, and they are more versatile and less hungry, and cleaner![5]

Since change is inevitable, we need to learn to embrace it as a value to be nurtured. Even change that at first blush appears to be negative may present us with a valuable opportunity. At the same time, it is important to keep in mind that change for the sake of change is little more than worthless!

Many times we find ourselves fighting change rather than accepting it or creating it because we're afraid of losing something we care about, something familiar that is more comfortable and less threatening than something we know little or nothing about. In *Transitions: Making Sense of Life's Changes,* William Bridges says that he sees three steps in dealing with change.[6]

Bridges's first step is *letting go or ending*. In any change—positive or negative—something is lost, so we have to take the time to let go, to make peace with the past, to recognize that what we had was good.

His second step is the *transition*. In this stage we feel as though we have lost control. We are in an unfamiliar situation—we wonder if we will be successful. We experience anxiety and confusion. We want everything to be as it was: neat, clean, and settled. In this stage we are searching for the meaning in the change. Negativity and anger are normal in this stage and should be expected.

His third step is *starting something new*. This stage can be frightening, enlightening, or a mixture of both. It is the exciting time when we see the benefits of accepting or implementing the dynamics of the new situation.

You may think that these stages are true only when change is imposed upon us. However, I would argue that they apply whether we are caught in changes created by others or are ourselves the creators of the change.

Each time I am the creator of change, or become involved in a changing environment, I find that I experience the three stages of change outlined by Bridges. Whether the changes are personal (that is, involve your own growth and development), are generated by you as a leader, or are environmentally imposed, you may find yourself dealing with anxiety, excitement, or doubt. That is normal. Change is never easy. If we are to create the future rather than be pushed into it, we need to anticipate change. We need to be trend watchers, sorting out fad from reality, always aware of the difficulties involved in accepting change. We need to be leaders of change.

I acknowledge that not all change is positive. We may find that at times the changes that evolve around us have a negative effect on our behavior and sense of values. For example, Raydean Acevedo, whom I have spoken about in an earlier chapter, finds the present-day regulatory, litigious environment concerning sexual harassment very stifling. She believes that it has introduced a level of anxiety into the workplace that is uncalled for. Let me hasten to add that she strongly agrees with the basis for the introduction of the regulations and laws, but believes that many people have overreacted to them. Raydean is Latina; she has grown up hugging and touching people as a part of her style of communication. Now she feels that she must be extremely guarded to avoid a misinterpretation of her style. This has introduced an uncomfortable level of stiffness into her communication with others. In the past, when a personal conflict had arisen with one of her employees, her first reaction had been to meet with the individual to talk about the problem. Now when a conflict is presented, she must first contact a legal representative and may not have a conversation with the employee until a witness is in the room. Raydean said, "It is a sad commentary on our present society to have to constantly walk on 'interpersonal eggshells.'"

Change is often a very painful experience. We find ourselves in unfamiliar situations, we fear failure, we grow anxious and critical. Fear of failure is one of the major causes of stress for people in leadership positions. A leader should have the courage to welcome an occasional failure. Some failures can be recognized as a sign that the individual or group is addressing change, is trying new approaches, setting ambitious goals, attempting to be creative. The greatest enemy of change, the biggest obstacle to innovation, is the lack of courage to take a risk. Those who wish to play it safe—make no changes—cannot hope to be the creative, courageous, forward-looking leaders of the future. I thoroughly enjoyed reading Tom Peters's book, *Thriving on Chaos,* from which I paraphrase the following advice:

How to Break Down Barriers to Innovation

1. Publicly applaud at least one failure (one that eventually led to a better way of doing things.)
2. Reward at least one act of *constructive* defiance.
3. Knock down at least one seemingly trivial barrier in a team's way.
4. Perform at least one small facilitating act.[7]

Being prepared for tomorrow's complicated, changing world requires us to courageously reach out with new experiments, new ideas, and risky possibilities that promise to improve our organization or community. Some attempts at addressing change may fail, but others will inevitably lead to powerful new ways to bring about a better society.

Wherever we are experiencing change, our values, communication skills, and vision become very important. Common values tie together the processes, the discussions, and the shared vision that create the bond of trust among those involved in the change. Coping with change, like the other links in the chain of effective leadership, takes practice. With each attempt to deal with change successfully, our thought and action processes become more resilient.

Personal Change

It has been said that it is the ultimate hypocrisy to demand of your team or organization things you won't do yourself; but changing yourself is absolutely one of the hardest things on earth to do. Habits from childhood are deeply embedded. Vested interests in certain attitudes and values get in the way of modifying behavior. And often the motivation to change is absent. However, communities and organizations will have a hard time renewing themselves if their leadership has stagnated!

A rather amazing example of personal change is the story of John Michael Talbot.[8] John was born a Methodist in Oklahoma City. At the age of ten he began displaying a talent for music by strumming his brother's guitar. At the age of fifteen he was playing the guitar in his brother's rock group. Although the group never achieved star billing, it produced five albums and appeared with just about all the big name acts of its era. Once after a concert, John remembers looking out over a big arena floor littered with empty wine and whiskey bottles and drug paraphernalia. He said, "Did I want this to be what my life stands for?"

While other band members got stoned in the back of the bus, he began paging through his grandmother's Bible. He did not want to give up his music, so he desperately began looking for a lifestyle that would allow him to express his musical talents in an environment with strong values. He tried fundamentalism but was unhappy with it, so he next tried Catholicism. This led to a radical life transition. Following the example of Saint Francis of Assisi, he sold everything he owned. He moved into a Catholic retreat center—and he didn't stop there.

He is now Brother John Michael Talbot and has become very successful in what he calls his "music ministry." Some consider him the male counterpart to Amy Grant, an award-winning Christian vocalist with a large pop music following. His thirty-fourth album is on the market and he is recognized as the biggest contemporary Roman Catholic sacred music star. If this appears to be a striking turn of events for a former rock musician—it is. Personal change is rarely so dramatic. However, whether our personal changes are small and incremental or as dramatic as John's, the manner in which we deal with them creates the outcome.

Here is another, less dramatic example of personal change. Maria (not her real name) is an extremely intelligent and gifted young woman. She loved her teaching position at a major university, and was constantly frustrated by what she perceived as the ineffectiveness of the other teachers in her department. At staff meetings she was aggressive, outspoken, and critical. Her reputation among students was stellar, but among the staff and administration she was considered a troublemaker. Finally, one of Maria's friends decided to confront her with the truth of her eroding popularity in the department. He gently but firmly told Maria that her style was causing more harm than good to herself and to her cause. He told her that if she wanted to create organizational change regarding students, she would first have to recognize the need to make some personal changes.

Maria was deeply hurt and angry, but she took the words of her friend to heart and began to seriously reflect on her behavior. She read several books on leadership and behavioral change. She participated in conflict resolution and personal development workshops and began practicing what she had learned. The results were amazing. The changes in her behavior were noticed. She began to get more invitations to serve on committees and other faculty groups than she could handle. She discovered that others were much more open to her suggestions and questions. Maria learned that by changing her behavior toward others she could become a leader for change at the university.

When dealing with personal change, we need to be willing to ask ourselves the same questions that are so useful when considering organizational change. Do you ever take the time to reflect on your strong opinions and beliefs and ask yourself if it might be useful to consider a change? Do you like learning and exploring new avenues? Do you believe that you should seek self-improvement? If your answer to these questions is yes, then some of your progress toward self-improvement and leadership development will be natural.

Exhibit 11.1 offers a list of factors that sometimes cause personal resistance to change. Read them, reflect on them, and then answer the questions that follow. This short exercise may help you recognize your personal roadblocks to change.

Organizational and Community Change

For any process of change—be it personal or organizational—to be effective over time, all the participants must share a vision, an understanding of the need for the change, and a sense of ownership in the change process. If the process and decision to change is viewed as imposed from above, the people of the community or organization will resent it and will slip back into old ways of doing things as soon as an opportunity presents itself. But if people believe that they have played a part in making the decision to change, they will commit to it and put energy into making sure that it works.

Open communication is essential to the process of change. If everyone understands the reasoning behind the request for change, they will understand the challenge and you will be sending a message that you respect their opinions, that they are trusted,

Exhibit 11.1. Spotting the Roadblocks.

Change-Resistance Factors

- Fear of the unknown
- Like it the way it is
- Fear of failure
- Not sure you have the proper training
- Too much effort required
- Fear of the loss of friends and colleagues
- Old habits are comfortable
- Fear of being forced to assume more responsibility

Which of these factors affect you the most? Select the top three that most clearly tell the story of why you resist change.

1. _____

2. _____

3. _____

Now take some time to reflect on how you can overcome at least one of these obstacles. If you did overcome this obstacle, what would be the outcome? What could you possibly gain?

Would you be more productive? Would you be exercising your leadership potential? Would you be of help to others? Would you increase the efficiency of everyone around you? Would you have better interpersonal relations?

_____

_____

_____

Good leaders are change agents who recognize that they are learning to address personal change while they are trying to successfully implement change in the world around them. In acknowledging your own need to grow and change, you have an opportunity to be a role model for others.

and that their support is needed. The easiest way to avoid resistance to change and keep people from viewing you as a manipulator is to involve all those individuals who will be affected by the change in the decision-making process. Give them all the information concerning why this change is necessary. Listen to what they have to say. You may even discover that someone else in your group or on your team has a far better idea for approaching the needed changes. Your ability to accept their recommendations and shelve your own ideas will build relationships and empower others as well as yourself in the process. Once again, the skill of weaving a shared vision is essential.

Be aware of a group's readiness to accept change, especially if you are promoting large-scale change. Regardless of the size of the community or organization, don't expect that everyone will be open to the level of change you are trying to promote. People are at different levels of risk taking and change acceptance. It is wisest to direct your change efforts to those groups or areas where energy for change already exists, rather than trying to convert the cynics and nay-sayers. Success by one group or team usually serves as a challenge to other groups. Sometimes pacing the change can be far more effective than trying to create a hurricane of change.

When the W.K. Kellogg Foundation decided to adopt a whole new system of technology that would involve cutting-edge tools and skills, the person in charge, Gail McClure, made a very wise decision. She recognized that there would be great resistance to another technological change, since there had already been one such change a year earlier. She requested that one team, the Kellogg National Fellowship Program (KNFP) team, serve as the experimental group to adopt and work with the new processes. This team was recognized as a group open to change, to new ideas and innovations.

The KNFP team accepted the challenge and served as guinea pigs for the many new and complicated processes and procedures. At times they were frustrated, but their insights helped improve the project and also assisted in the implementation of the new systems throughout the foundation. Had Gail imposed the new technologies on the entire foundation staff, she might have met with anger, cynicism, mass frustration—and possibly failure. By moving this radical change one step at a time, she helped the Kellogg Foundation succeed with the new technology.

Real Change or Paper Change?

As I travel about the country speaking to groups about leadership and community issues, I hear a lot of talk about organizations and communities as collections of systems and structures. "Systems change" has become an "in" phrase. People who are trying to change their communities, schools, hospitals, or workplaces bring charts and grids displaying change to our meetings and ask me to help them analyze them. They think they can effect systems change that will improve their circumstances as they move into the next century and improve personal relationships at the same time—by reengineering the organizational structure with the help of another new diagram. They design elaborate charts with little or no attention to the real issue: What motivates people to change and to succeed?

Leadership by grid, box, or chart can only get you so far! Change is an essentially human issue—it is people-centered rather than chart-centered. You can't simply rearrange boxes or draw them as circles or triangles and somehow expect that people will accept change and relate to each other differently. If you want your community or organization to accept change, to consider the "what could be" rather than the "what is," then your leadership must focus on people. Your community, school, or workplace will definitely accept change when people are recognized as the basic building blocks of the enterprise—no matter what that may be.

Ask yourself the following questions: How do I support the people who are working with me? Do they clearly understand the ramifications of their performance? Do I provide opportunities for them to learn new skills and behaviors? Are they prepared for the changes I am introducing? Am I good at giving positive and negative feedback? Do I share power and recognize, nurture, and develop leadership and followership skills in myself and others? Without a keen understanding of these people issues and interconnections, it is unlikely that any real systems change will take place.

With people as the center of the change activities, the organization or community begins to function as teams of people with a common goal and set of values. The boxes, grids, triangles, and circles may be enablers or inhibitors, but only people can be the driving force for change. Charts may serve as a pictorial display of efficiency or inefficiency, but they can never define how people behave.

Success for communities and organizations of the future will depend upon the collective knowledge of all the people involved. The energy, judgment, perceptions, experience, intuition, and intelligence of transforming leaders and loyal, supportive followers will be invaluable assets to communities or organizations as they adapt to the rapid pace of change we are all experiencing today.

One of the primary responsibilities of a person functioning as the leader of a group is defining reality. As definers of reality, leaders help establish an understanding about "what is" and "what could be." Open-mindedness, creativity, and initiative are three of the most useful attributes in this process. However, we already know that it isn't possible for one person to see all sides of a problem or issue and have absolute wisdom about possible solutions to problems that may be caused by change. Creating an atmosphere with strong, positive interpersonal dynamics, where anyone can speak up, is key to the process of effecting positive change. To introduce an innovation openly is not enough. Skillful leadership will encourage active dialogue and, in some cases, allow and encourage group decision making. Sometimes this means being prepared for some pretty heated debates. This can be very productive. Putting a lid on disagreements and public dialogue only interferes with the creative process. If that happens, there will be little innovation and only grudging compliance. Disagreement can either serve as a stimulant for innovation and change or as a source of hard feelings and anger, depending largely on the attitude and process skills of the group.

Change and renewal involves deliberate personal and organizational attention. If the leaders of the community or organization are truly interested in change, they will recognize the leadership talents of everyone involved. They will celebrate people! They will cultivate an environment that encourages individuality of ideas and organizational self-criticism, and will encourage the idea of fluidity and change for the organization.

Because of a basic belief in the power of ordinary people, one small town has gone through a remarkable metamorphosis. In 1991, the town of Eldorado, in rural southern Illinois, was a declining community. It was a community facing economic difficulties, loss of youth, an aging population, and the flight of most of the businesses that had kept it alive. Like the rest of its region, Eldorado had experienced coal mine closings, oil resource depletion, and agricultural depression. But Gene Rhine, a retired English teacher, was not about to allow his town to fade away.

He energetically assumed a leadership role and gathered a group of concerned citizens into an organization they named Eldorado Project Bounce—or Better Opportunity Under Noble Civic Efforts. They were determined to work to make their community bounce back. This group of citizens didn't wait for people with titles or positions of authority to take the lead; they were personally committed to determining the fate of their community, rather than awaiting the slow, agonizing decline typical of many small midwestern rural communities.

After the initial conflict and dialogue about which idea was best, each member of this group recognized that they all would have to be both leaders and followers if they were going to revitalize their town. The group worked hard to develop a shared vision that focused on changing Eldorado into a unique historical center of tourism and antique trade.

"The local Chamber of Commerce donated $5,000 for seed money. A former Eldorado woman . . . [anonymously] donated $10,000. A beautification committee put up . . . welcome banners, new park benches and planted trees. A ways and means committee organized monthly events. . . . An advertising committee drew up brochures that touted Eldorado as the 'City of Antiques, Arts, Crafts, [and] Specialty Shops.'"[9] All this activity was accomplished by volunteers.

They recruited many talented individuals to join their cause. As a result, Irene Muckley, the owner of an antique mall, wrote a proposal and received a grant to restore the Old City Hall, which has become the hub of activity. Sixteen new businesses were opened the first year and twenty-five additional small businesses opened during the second year of Project Bounce's existence. As a result of several of the volunteer projects, the community received Illinois Governor James Edgar's award for economic improvement and earned recognition in *Midwest Living* magazine with an Honor Roll of Hometown Pride award.[10]

Eldorado has indeed bounced back! Perhaps it would be more accurate to say that Eldorado's citizens were successful in creating the future. Gene Rhine and the hundreds of young and old volunteers are extremely proud of what they have accomplished in the past four years. These citizens recognized that change is inevitable; they found their voice and took action. "If we didn't have Project Bounce, [Eldorado] would be a ghost town, I believe," said Don Davis, a retired grocer who has now opened The Deli in downtown Eldorado.[11] Gene Rhine may have served as the original organizer, but the events that followed were a reflection of the true meaning of *citizen leadership*.

The *In Context* quarterly tells us:

> Community-based change is fast becoming the key to America's future. More and more, local communities across the country are mobilizing their own resources in sustainable and creative ways to meet the needs of their members. From affordable housing and neighborhood enterprises to recreation and recycling, communities are finding that the best way to seek change is to organize. . . .

> This change in perspective is a clean departure from the American habit of looking to public policy, social services, and the market system for solutions to endemic problems like homelessness, unemployment, and pollution. Citizens all over are realizing that *they* must take the lead in addressing these problems instead of waiting for the country's leaders to take the initiative.[12]

Anticipating change is a serious leadership responsibility as we approach a new century. I would encourage you to reflect on your openness to change in the many different environments in which you operate. Another important factor to consider while reflecting on change is your attitude and ability to handle stress. *Change does cause stress.* Sometimes we need to inject some humor into our situation as we struggle to deal with the many serious implications of developing leadership and followership skills. If we allow ourselves to become stressed out by trying to achieve perfection, we'll wear out before we achieve our goals. In the next chapter, I will share some ideas about how we can alleviate stress and create a dynamic environment through the use of humor and fun.

Chapter Twelve

Humor Works

Effective leaders usually can tell a joke, take a joke, and
tell a good story.
—THOMAS E. CRONIN

Have you ever heard of a "humor consultant"? In Ft. Collins, Colorado, C. W. Metcalf (a forty-two-year-old former hospice worker, teacher, writer, and mime) has found a unique line of work: "humor, risk, and change adaptation—a serious look at the benefits of humor in the workplace." He adds, "Humor flies in the face of a lot of old-line thinking, that, if you're serious about your job, you're here 60 hours a week, and there's no place for laughter and silliness. It's got to the point where if we're enjoying our job, we must be doing something *wrong*. Stress has become the red badge of courage." Metcalf believes that whether in the workplace or in our communities, the primary cause of stress and illness related to stress is rapid change—and that a sense of humor is one of the inherent abilities we all possess to cope with this stress.[1]

You have now read many pages of why and what you need to do to achieve effective leadership. Leadership is serious stuff; it is hard work, right? Do you agree that leaders should be encouraged to have fun? Should organizations expect or allow humor and celebration in the workplace? Should you encourage your team or volunteer group to take time out to celebrate a birthday, a success, an engagement, or other similar occasions? Or are you one of those individuals who believe that humor, like a comfortable sweatshirt, should be stashed in the closet and saved for weekends?[2]

Humor as Tension Breaker

Many people are uncomfortable with the terms *fun* and *humor* when they are discussing leadership in their jobs or some project they are trying to accomplish in their communities. They associate fun and humor with lack of concentration, frivolousness, or kids' stuff. But I assure you that these two words, fun *and* humor, have a very important place in everything we do, as well as in maintaining our health and well-being.

I have a friend who holds a very stressful executive position. He travels extensively and interacts with a wide variety of powerful people in the United States and abroad. He is committed to his job—and to his wife and daughters, who wish he were home more often. His excellent sense of humor has carried him through many difficult situations.

However, as he approached his fiftieth birthday he amazed everyone by expressing deep concern about the process of aging. The thought of being fifty made him very uncomfortable. His staff decided to help relieve his stress by giving him a rousing party that would also point out the alternative. They knew he always appreciated a good laugh and a chance for fun. They planned the usual food and fun-filled birthday party, but they also included a lesson on life. On the day of his birthday, they draped his office in black, put dead plants in his flower pots, wrote an obituary, and played a funeral march as he walked into the office. Oh, how he laughed—and what a birthday party they all had! He got their message! He realized that the alternative to turning fifty wasn't acceptable and he joined whole-heartedly in the celebration.

He had cultivated an atmosphere of fun and hard work among his staff so that they felt free to tease him and to take the time to celebrate. Their surprise party relieved his distress over aging and everyone had a good time. It is also important to note that the organization where he is employed approves of such celebrations and encourages employees to find time to relieve stress through celebrations and fun.

Humor is not only an effective stress reducer, it can also serve as a very potent motivator. Whether you are leading a Girl Scout troop, a classroom, a project team, a company, or a city, a constant sense of optimism, a good sense of humor, and the ability to inspire others are critical characteristics for success.

Let's stop a minute to take a broad view of our day-to-day activities. Most people's lives are roughly divided into thirds—one third sleeping, one third (usually much more) working at home or at a place of employment, and one third worrying about the work that must be done and trying to learn how to relax! If you happen to have a restless night and sleep poorly, have a less than satisfying encounter with your family, and then must also interact with a humorless boss or group of colleagues at work, you could be well on the way to a shortened life span, as well as to total nonproductivity. In reality, humor may be one of the most inexpensive and readily available nonprescription medications to reduce stress, stimulate creativity, and improve performance. Why don't we make better use of it? Why do we save it for those rare occasions when we are on vacation or having a Sunday evening card game with family or friends? Where have we learned that fun and work or study are not to be mixed?

In *A Passion for Excellence,* Peters and Austin divulge a secret theory. They hypothesize that above every professional school entrance there must be a giant stone lintel deeply engraved with the following: *"All ye who enter here shall never smile again. American business/education/etc. is damned serious stuff!"*[3] Whether this indoctrination to avoid fun has taken place in our schools, our homes, or our workplaces, it appears to be a prevalent state of mind. Yet time and again we have all observed that winners are people who have fun and who encourage fun and humor among others. They laugh easily—at themselves and with others. A very popular dentist in our town had a huge sign at the entry to his office. It read: "We cater to cowards!" Almost every single person who walked through that door smiled, no matter how serious the toothache or how dreadful the fear of dentists. This dentist had a long waiting list of patients and a thriving business despite the pain he inevitably caused along the way. His jovial personality was reflected not only in the way he conducted his business, but in everything he did. Such leaders produce results and spur enthusiasm as an outcome of their zest and optimism. They motivate people with their energy and willingness to celebrate the successes of others.

Laughter is always free. It helps build relationships and is usually harmless. Of course, ethnic jokes, racial and sexist slurs, or putdowns cannot be considered acceptable humor. In the worst-case scenario, they are mean-spirited and totally unacceptable; at best, they are thoughtless and irresponsible. However, making fun of yourself or something you have done with self-deprecating humor can break down many barriers. It lets us laugh *with* each other rather than *at* each other. If you happen to be a supervisor, it helps those working with you to catch a glimpse of you as a real person. Wouldn't we all take a giant step toward success if we would attempt to create an environment at home and at work where everyone looks forward to a new day and a new challenge?

Remember Father Bill Cunningham and Eleanor Josaitis, the people from Detroit? They obviously had to have a marvelous sense of humor to suggest a street party to divert a racial explosion in their city. Most people would have suggested armed guards and a curfew! Armed guards might have aroused anger and resentment, but the street party threw everyone off guard. People didn't expect it, it tickled their funny bone, and they decided to join in the fun.

Here is another example of using humor as a tool for success. A consultant hired to help an organization solve its communication problems startled everyone at the first meeting by asking: "How can we be sure to have absolutely rotten communication around here?" The group immediately relaxed and got into the spirit of the question, pelting her with answers: "Make sure everyone works in total isolation." "Never smile or say hello in the morning." "Make all memos long, boring, and irrelevant." She says, "This brainstorming approach never fails to evoke laughter as well as a lively discussion. When you turn the statements around ('make sure no one works in isolation') the solutions become obvious."[4]

Work groups or project teams often focus single-mindedly on the task at hand and discourage any activity that might appear less than deeply serious. In fact, with some groups, seriousness replaces Godliness as a virtue! But if you look around, you will most likely note that the most effective teams are those that both encourage humor and celebrate the successes of their members. That is not to say that failures are ignored or disregarded. Rather, the group members support each other in taking risks that at times will produce less than positive results.

"Researchers exploring the uses of humor have found that making fun of life's problems and our reactions to them can help us tolerate those problems for longer periods of time. Humor can be a tension breaker, a mood lifter, a relationship mender, and a pain reliever."[5]

Humor as Energizer

Leadership requires an openness to change; in fact, as I have said, leaders are agents of change. When trying to effect change of any significance, it is inevitable that some extremely stressful, serious barriers will be encountered. Even projects that at first glance appear very simple and sensible may present difficulties that are impossible to foresee. Often these roadblocks are bureaucratic or political. Getting over, around, or through these barriers to achieve the necessary change can demand extraordinary energy and effort. With anything less than highly motivated individuals, these barriers can destroy an entire change effort or slow it to a snail's pace. Humor can serve as a valuable asset to release the tension and stress created in such situations. It can stimulate the mental and physical energy needed to complete the task, and can help restore sagging morale.

Achieving extraordinary visions despite obstacles always requires an occasional burst of energy. Such energy can be cultivated and nurtured by certain motivational and inspirational processes that include humor, celebration, personal recognition, and respect. Rather than controlling, commanding, or pushing people in the direction of the vision, leaders who understand stress and the value of humor direct their attention to very basic human needs. These needs may include achievement, belonging, recognition, self-esteem, a sense of control over one's life, living up to one's ideals, and ultimately, being part of the group or team responsible not only for achieving, but for developing the vision.

An important function of a leader is the ability to generate this highly energized behavior, or see to it that there is someone on the team who can do so. This skill is almost as important as understanding yourself and finding your voice, as being able to develop a shared vision, as recognizing that loyal followership is as important as leadership, and that trust is something that is earned. In fact, all these factors fit together into a very neat, comprehensive package.

Think of it this way: developing a shared vision identifies an appropriate path for movement, effective followership aligns the group and gets them moving down the path, and a successful motivational effort assures that the team will have the energy, joy, and *fun* necessary to overcome the obstacles on their way to their goal.

Any of you who have participated in a team sport will readily recognize the effectiveness of this model. Have you ever considered using this model in other life situations as well? Someone once told me that to be a success, I needed to have a hearty laugh at least once a day—and not a giggle but a good old-fashioned belly laugh. No matter how hectic the pace of life, I find that whenever I forget this wise advice I become buried in anxiety and plagued by stress attacks. Obviously life isn't filled with belly laughs, but neither should it be drowned in tears of stress! I'm certain that you can readily recognize the human weakness of making mountains out of molehills. The successful person is one who puts things into perspective, who maintains a sense of balance.

Managing Stress

It is neither an embarrassment nor a weakness to admit that stress does exist in our daily lives. Most of us have to deal with some or all of these stress factors: massive cutbacks and layoffs affecting our own industry or our customers, longer work days, violence in our cities, the need to juggle jobs and family responsibilities—and the list goes on indefinitely. If you are in a leadership position where your power is derived from a title or a box on an organizational chart, you may find the new concepts of flattened organizations and roving leadership extremely stressful as well. These examples can be termed *negative stress,* but not all stress is negative. There is also such a thing as *creative stress*—the kind that gives us a rush or high and contributes to our energy level and motivation. Although most of the factors listed above contribute to our distress, it is also important to keep in mind that there is such a thing as creative tension or stress.

Distress can become a significant inhibiting factor, affecting our health and productivity. It contributes generously to the physical and mental wear and tear we experience in our lives. High blood pressure, ulcers, and heart and digestive problems are just a few illnesses associated with negative stress. So what can we do about it? How can we learn to accept situations as they are and take steps to keep ourselves and our colleagues healthy and productive?

Because the consequences of distress can involve low productivity, absenteeism, poor decision making, and increased health care costs, many companies and organizations are providing employees with an opportunity to participate in stress-management programs. These programs can take a variety of forms. The most radical approach is to hire a humor consultant like C. W. Metcalf. Yes, believe it or not, companies and organizations are resorting to this measure, and not just in northern Colorado. Research is suggesting that perhaps the negative effects of stress can be mitigated through laughter. According to Steve Allen Jr., a family physician and associate dean of student affairs for the College of Medicine at the State University of New York in Syracuse, "Some studies indicate that people are more creative when they are having fun, and trust increases when they are laughing together."[6] These last two factors, creativity and trust, are invaluable to any organization. It might well be worth the cost of hiring a humor consultant to achieve them. You may reject the idea, labeling it artificial, but with the multiple stress factors in all our environments, it may be a necessity.

An example of using humor as a stress reliever is the "Humor Room." "One CEO converted her company's sick room—a place for people who were feeling ill to lie down—into a room full of cartoons, videos and books intended to make stressed-out employees laugh. The same CEO is redecorating her boardroom with humorous posters—to make it less of a 'bored' room, she says."[7]

Regular exercise is another personal approach to handling stress. Any exercise that increases the heart rate is most beneficial. Even a quick walk in the fresh air often helps release mounting tension or anger caused by stress. Some organizations have resorted to providing on-site fitness centers to help their employees manage the stress of their everyday lives.

Taking your community group or a group of employees out of their familiar setting and placing them in a more relaxed environment for work or brainstorming sessions is also a very effective means of building relationships and easing tensions. Sometimes these activities are called *retreats*. These can simply be working meetings held in a place with beautiful, restful surroundings. Alternatively, they can be highly structured activities such as Outward

Bound or the Ropes Courses that are designed specifically to challenge the group to work together to solve problems.

Sometimes we allow ourselves to become so busy with work or business challenges that we forget the joy of little things. Many organizations today are choosing to put an emphasis on celebration to relieve the stress of day-to-day demands and to introduce a positive spirit into the workplace. Organizational celebration is a way of honoring individuals, groups, events, achievements, the common and the ordinary happenings in the lives of people in a creative and often festive manner. Celebration is also a very effective way to build relationships within an organization or community.

Traditional celebrations usually include banquets, picnics, birthdays, annual dinners, honors, retirements, and other events that mark significant moments for people in the group. Wise leaders know that people often let their defenses down as they relax and enjoy an event. Leaders who encourage conscious celebrations find that the individuals involved tend to form deeper relationships, become more open to creative ideas, and exhibit a willingness to share power. These celebrations can become healing high-touch events in a world that has become very remote and high-tech.

In the end, we all need to recognize that stress is a very individual issue. What is stressful to one person can be energizing to another. I, for example, love public speaking. Participating in a public forum as a speaker energizes me and keeps me on a high for days. I have friends who absolutely dread speaking before any size group. The tension and stress they experience when forced into this activity are formidable. Their appetite, sleep, and relationships are all negatively affected by the occasion. Each person has his or her own list of negative or positive stress factors. It is impossible for us to eliminate all stress from our lives, but we can either avoid the occasions that cause extreme stress or we can learn to manage stress for successful outcomes.

There are entire books written on stress management. You will find some of these books listed in Resource B. Common sense tells us that people function better and make better decisions when they are fit and having fun. As you prepare to be the best that you can be as both a creative leader and a loyal, supportive follower, try to remember the importance of having fun and recognizing the different stress levels of those with whom you work. Remember, *"Laughter is the sun that drives winter from the human face."*[8]

Chapter Thirteen

Summoning the Courage to Act

Tell me and I'll forget; show me and I may remember;
involve me and I'll understand.
—CHINESE PROVERB

The challenges for our generation and the next are numerous and demanding. Everything I have shared with you in this book and more will be necessary to help us move positively toward the next century. In the first section, I dealt with inner motivation and tried to persuade you that you do not need a title or position to be a leader. I hope I made my point so well with examples and ideas that you are ready and energized to take up the challenge. I also stressed the importance of knowing yourself through reflection and self-observation. In the second section, I dealt with the essential aspects of effective leadership including:

- *Weaving a shared vision* of the goals, dreams, and hopes of independent persons into a vital, shared vision that responds to the common good.
- *Viewing the world through the kaleidoscope* of cultural and gender differences and viewpoints.
- *Communicating with meaning* and acquiring the skills of active, positive listening.
- *Maintaining ethics and trust* in deciding how to decide.
- *Taking risks* and being open to change.
- *Balancing power and compassion.*

- *Recognizing that change is inevitable* and must be anticipated and managed.
- *Using humor and managing stress* to alleviate tension and create joy in your work or home environment.

Now there is one more step that we need to take as we work together toward more effective leadership. That step is developing the courage to take action: the ability to make it happen, to translate your passion into reality, to develop a plan of action and produce results.

Knowing ourselves and how we are unique, finding our voice, and discovering what we need to do to improve are important factors to consider as we set out on our journey of leadership development and begin producing results. Obviously this book and the limited number of exercises we can provide are not sufficient; no single resource is. However, the short exercises that follow may stimulate your desire to learn more about yourself and more about the process of effective leadership. To pursue the matter further, see the Resources section that follows this chapter.

Personal Leadership Development Goals

In Chapters Five through Twelve, you studied and read about many outstanding people who are exemplars of the essential elements of effective citizen leadership. I am sure that one or two of these examples have encouraged you to think about some attitudinal and behavioral changes that you might make to improve your own effectiveness as a leader. Some of these changes can be achieved in a relatively short period of time. Others may take longer. Whether short-term or long-term, don't put your goals off. Start now!

Complete the short- and long-term goal chart in Exhibit 13.1. *Be sure to think carefully about your projected date for completion.* Be realistic, but don't be too easy on yourself. Each of these goals is based on the essential aspects of leadership discussed in Chapters Five through Twelve. Be sure that your goals are specific and measurable. For example, to say "I will be open to many points of view" is an aspiration, not a measurable goal. In measurable terms, it might be stated as "For the next three months, at the end of meetings with my team, committee, or family, I will ask the group whether they felt that I have heard all points of view on the topic we are discussing."

Exhibit 13.1. Goals Worksheet.

| *Short-Term Goals* | *(Date)* | *Long-Term Goals* | *(Date)* |

Weaving a Shared Vision

Example: I will invite others with whom I work to share their personal visions with me.   (9/1/97)

Together we will work to weave all of the personal visions into a shared vision that responds to the common good.   (1/1/98)

_____

_____

Openness to Many Points of View

_____

_____

Communication and Listening

_____

_____

Decision Making

_____

_____

Risk Taking

_____

_____

Balancing Power and Compassion

_____

_____

Serving as a Change Agent

_____

_____

Using Humor and Handling Stress

_____

_____

After you have completed this goal exercise, you may want to clip it out or photocopy it and put it in a place where you will see it daily. Frequent reminders will keep you moving from "what is" toward "what could be."

Action Takes Planning

You have now dealt with how you plan to improve or develop your leadership skills. These are all self-development goals. You may choose to work on only one or two of them at a time. Now turn back to Exhibit 2.1, where I asked you to prioritize the social, organizational, or family issues that were most important to you. Do you still agree with what you wrote there? If so, use the issue you placed in column C for the exercise in Exhibit 13.2. I want you to develop a plan that will outline the steps you will take to do something positive about this issue. Whether you choose to assume a leadership role or that of a loyal, supportive follower is inconsequential. *What is important is that you do something to make a difference.*

Try to plan your leadership action with passion, enthusiasm, love, and commitment. However, no plan of action is complete unless you have also developed a means to evaluate your success. I'll leave that process to your creativity and initiative. In the end, remember, the measure of your success will not be whether you functioned as a leader or a follower, whether you finished the project on time, whether you spent too much money, or whether everyone agreed that this was a top priority. The measure of your success will be your ability to answer the simple question, *so what?* So what was different because you completed this project? What did you expect to learn from it? Did others benefit? Is your community, family, or workplace better as a result? You have almost finished this book and you have given some thought to how you can make a difference. Now it is up to you to carry out the task you have said needs to be done.

Conclusion

Eleanor Josaitis and Father Bill Cunningham can see, feel, and measure the difference they have made in the city of Detroit. Sarah, the teenager from New England, has experienced the pleasure and

Exhibit 13.2. Action Plan Worksheet.

Issue

Please begin your plan by answering the following questions:

- What action can I take over the next two or three months to improve the situation or have an impact on this issue?

  _____

  _____

  _____

- What skills do I still need to develop so as to address the issue more effectively?

  _____

  _____

  _____

- What will be different if I follow through with this action?

  _____

  _____

  _____

- How will I evaluate the results of this action?

  _____

  _____

  _____

pain of leadership as an organizer who has affected the lives of children in a domestic violence center. Walter Turnbull has changed the lives of hundreds of African American boys. These individuals and the many others found in the pages of this book are leaders. As you know, most of them do not have titles or positions of authority, but they have had the courage to take action on an issue that was important to them. From their often humble beginnings, from their courage and values, and from what they have been able to accomplish, there are many lessons to learn. We need only to look around us to recognize many more outstanding models of the creative process. With imagination, courage, and commitment, these people have transcended fear, insecurity, feelings of powerlessness, and lack of money or positions of power, and they have achieved outstanding results.

During your life, you will find many people like those you have read about in this book whose actions will encourage and support you. In the process of succeeding, they have all suffered setbacks, failures, and disappointments. They have used what they learned from such situations to become better leaders and achieve even greater outcomes. Ultimately, however, all must make their own decisions. You will have to set the standards for your own success. You will have to take the steps necessary to get to know who you are, to find your voice, and then to develop your strengths so that you can make a difference as a leader or as a loyal, supportive follower. Others may inspire and be role models for you, but in the end, you will need to trust your own sense of what is right for you.

Good luck as you venture into the world of effective leadership. It will be hard work, but as you succeed—and sometimes fail—just remember this advice:

> When Pablo Casals was ninety years old, the greatest of all cellists, he kept practicing the cello for four or five hours each day. Someone asked him why, at his age, he worked so hard at the fundamentals of his art. "Because," he said, "I think I am making some progress."
>
> Life is really all about making some progress at being what we are meant to be—the way being a bud is about becoming a blossom, or being a well-born colt is about becoming a thoroughbred

racer. We have an inner itch to be more of what we were meant to be, and we never know but that we are on the verge of a breakthrough.[1]

In summary, allow me to remind you that in a democracy every citizen has the option and the responsibility to be a part of the process of improving society. With your help, we can reshape the thinking about leadership and followership so that more and more of us can find and use our voices to serve others and to create a brighter future for those who follow us.

Resources

Whenever you are asked if you can do a job, tell 'em,
"Certainly I can!" Then get busy and find out how
to do it.
—THEODORE ROOSEVELT

The people you have met in this book have made positive contributions to their communities, families, or workplaces. In some cases they made mistakes. It took all of them a great deal of effort and dedication. I am convinced that most people are excited and willing to make a difference. What we need to be more effective contributors to our society are encouragement, examples, education, and training. The following pages are only a first step to the lifelong process of learning that can make us vibrant, contributing members of society.

Peter Senge, who has done extensive work on the topic of building learning organizations, tells us:

> Human beings are designed for learning. No one has to teach an infant to walk, or talk, or master the spatial relationships needed to stack eight building blocks that don't topple. Children come fully equipped with an insatiable drive to explore and experiment. Unfortunately, the primary institutions of our society are oriented predominantly toward controlling rather than learning, rewarding individuals for performing for others rather than for cultivating their natural curiosity and impulse to learn. The young child entering school discovers quickly that the name of the game is getting the right answer and avoiding mistakes—a mandate no less compelling to the aspiring manager.[1]

Few things that are worthwhile in this life are learned in a single day, a week, or a month. Certainly, learning the art of leadership is

161

a lifelong challenge. All of us must keep on learning. We must keep our minds open—be receptive to new ideas—understand that in an increasingly dynamic, interdependent, and unpredictable world, it is simply not possible for any one person to have all the answers. Today and tomorrow demand that we rely on integrating thinking, learning, and acting at all levels of our society.

People who allow themselves to get so busy that they resign themselves to just doing their jobs—who don't open themselves to new ideas and new developments and who refuse to take the risk to learn new things—will look around some day and find themselves out of step with their times.

If you have found your voice and I have captured your imagination with your potential to learn to lead more effectively, then the following pages may serve as a rich resource as you implement your action plan. The lists of leadership development programs, books, audiotapes, videotapes, and films that you will find here all speak in some meaningful way to leadership skills and development.

If you want to build your ability and skills in leadership, it is not enough to read one or two books on the subject, or to attend a single leadership seminar. There is a growing wealth of knowledge in the field of leadership that is largely untapped by potential citizen leaders like you. This waste of resources must change, for I firmly believe it is the responsibility of each and every one of us to put this information to its greatest use. I encourage you to immerse yourself in these materials. Each one of them is an excellent source not only of information but also of strength and encouragement. Learn from them; practice them; enjoy them. But use them only as a starting block, then venture out on your own.

Resource A

Leadership Development Programs

Advocacy Institute Leadership Development Program
1707 L Street N.W., Fourth Floor
Washington DC 20036
(202) 659–8475 FAX: (202) 659–8484

American Leadership Forum
P.O. Box 3689
Stanford CA 94309
(415) 723–6127 FAX: (415) 723–6131

Center for Community Change
1000 Wisconsin Avenue N.W.
Washington DC 20007
(202) 342–0519 FAX: (202) 342–1132

Center for Creative Leadership
One Leadership Place
P.O. Box 26300
Greensboro NC 27438
(910) 288–7210 FAX: (910) 288–3999

Community Development Institute Leadership Training Academy
321 Bell Street
P.O. Box 50099
East Palo Alto CA 94303
(415) 327–5846 FAX: (415) 327–4430

Community Training and Assistance Center
30 Winter Street, Seventh Floor
Boston MA 02108
(617) 423–1444 FAX: (617) 423–4748

Coro Southern California Neighborhood Leadership Program
811 Wilshire Boulevard, Suite 1025
Los Angeles CA 90017
(213) 623–1234 FAX: (213) 680–0079

Development Training Institute
2500 Maryland Avenue
Baltimore MD 21218
(410) 338–2512 FAX: (410) 338–2751

Disney University Professional Development Programs
P.O. Box 10093
Lake Buena Vista FL 32830–0093
(407) 824–4855 FAX: (407) 824–4866

Future Leaders of America
1110 Camellia Street
Oxnard CA 93030
(805) 485–5237 or 385–2676 FAX: (805) 485–5237

Grassroots Leadership
1300 Baxter Street, Suite 200
P.O. Box 36006
Charlotte NC 28236
(704) 332–3090 FAX: (704) 332–0445

Heartland Center for Leadership Development
941 O Street, Suite 920
Lincoln NE 68508
(402) 474–7667 FAX: (402) 474–7672

Highlander Research and Education Center
1959 Highlander Way
New Market TN 37820
(615) 933–3443 FAX: (615) 933–3424

Indian Dispute Resolution Services, Inc.
1029 K Street, Suite 38
Sacramento CA 95814
(916) 447–4800 FAX: (916) 447–4808

Innovation Associates, Inc.
Three Speen Street, Suite 140
Framingham MA 01701
(508) 879–8301 FAX: (508) 626–2205

Institute for Educational Leadership, Inc.
1001 Connecticut Avenue N.W., Suite 310
Washington DC 20036
(202) 822–8405 FAX: (202) 872–4050

Kellogg International Leadership Program
    and Kellogg National Fellowship Program
W.K. Kellogg Foundation
One Michigan Avenue East
Battle Creek MI 49017–4058
(616) 968–1611 FAX: (616) 968–0413

Leadership Education for Asian Pacifics
327 East Second Street, Suite 226
Los Angeles CA 90012
(213) 485–1422 FAX: (213) 485–0050

National Association for Community Leadership
200 South Meridian Street, Suite 340
Indianapolis IN 46225
(317) 637–7408 FAX: (317) 637–7413

National Hispana Leadership Institute
1901 North Moore, Suite 206
Arlington VA 22209
(703) 527–6007 FAX: (703) 527–6009

Outward Bound National Headquarters
    Professional Development Programs
Route 9D
R2, Box 280
Garrison NY 10524–9757
(914) 424–4000 or (800) 243–8520 FAX: (914) 424–4280

Princeton Center for Leadership Training
997 Lenox Drive, Suite 304
Lawrenceville NJ 08648
(609) 844–1040 FAX: (609) 844–1011

Program for Community Problem Solving
915 15th Street N.W., Suite 600
Washington DC 20005
(202) 783–2961 FAX: (202) 347–2161

Robert K. Greenleaf Center for Servant-Leadership
921 East 86th Street, Suite 200
Indianapolis IN 46240
(317) 259–1241 FAX: (317) 259–0560

Wisconsin Rural Development Center
1406 Business Highway 18/151
Mount Horeb WI 53572–9981
(608) 437–5971 FAX: (608) 437–5972

Recommended Books on Leadership

The Adventure of Leadership. Hap Klopp with Brian Tarcy. Stamford, Conn.: Longmeadow Press, 1991. Through the use of stories that both entertain and inform, this book challenges some of the conventional ideas about leadership and management.

Authentic Leadership. Robert W. Terry. San Francisco: Jossey-Bass, 1993. Offers an in-depth discussion of past and present views of leadership, then presents Terry's contention that leadership is a type of action, with the central principle being authenticity.

Beyond the Myths and Magic of Mentoring. Margo Murray with Marna A. Owen. San Francisco: Jossey-Bass, 1991. Provides step-by-step guidelines for fostering successful mentoring relationships in organizations and shows the various forms such mentoring programs can take by discussing seven case examples.

Choosing to Lead. Kenneth E. Clark and Miriam B. Clark. Charlotte, N.C.: Leadership Press, 1994. Makes the argument that for leaders to be effective, they must not only be aware of the required responsibilities of and commitment to leadership but they must first and foremost make a conscious decision to lead. The final chapter lists 127 statements on leadership—the result of the authors' many years of research.

Church Leadership. Lovett H. Weems Jr. Nashville, Tenn.: Abingdon Press, 1993. In an effort to assist church leaders in their attempts to create a positive environment of change, Weems identifies four crucial elements of effective church leadership: vision, team, culture, and integrity.

The Classic Touch. John K. Clemens and Douglas F. Mayer. Homewood, Ill.: Dow Jones-Irwin, 1987. Applies the lessons learned in the classic works of Western philosophy, history, biography, and drama to the modern dilemmas faced by managers and leaders today.

Collaborative Leadership. David D. Chrislip and Carl E. Larson. San Francisco: Jossey-Bass, 1994. Provides an insightful view of how communities can effect meaningful and lasting change through the collaboration of its diverse members, while explaining specific leadership strategies necessary for successful collaboration.

Credibility. James M. Kouzes and Barry Z. Posner. San Francisco: Jossey-Bass, 1993. Based on a vast number of surveys, case studies, and interviews, this book reveals six disciplines related to developing and sustaining credibility, which, the authors argue, is the key to leadership.

Even Eagles Need a Push. David McNally. New York: Delacorte Press, 1990. An inspiring book designed to help you take charge of your life and discover your true sense of purpose relating to your work life, personal life, and overall happiness.

Excellence. John W. Gardner. New York: Norton, 1984. A revised version of the original 1961 work, this book raises questions that all U.S. citizens should be asking themselves concerning issues of equality, the educational system, the nature of leadership in a democratic society, and above all, under what conditions excellence is possible in our society.

The Female Advantage. Sally Helgesen. New York: Doubleday, 1990. Offers an uncommon look at leadership through observations of four women leaders, discussing the differences in the way women— in contrast to men—manage and lead, and the strengths found in these differences.

The Fifth Discipline. Peter M. Senge. New York: Doubleday, 1990. Using examples drawing on science, spiritual wisdom, psychology, and top corporations, Senge offers a unique perspective and discusses the five disciplines that, once mastered, can enable organizations to overcome learning disabilities and become true learning organizations.

First Things First. Stephen R. Covey, Roger A. Merrill, and Rebecca R. Merrill. New York: Simon & Schuster, 1994. Applies the insights learned in *The Seven Habits of Highly Effective People* to the everyday struggle to balance the demands of work and personal life, looking at time management in a very nontraditional way.

Getting Things Done When You Are Not in Charge. Geoffrey M. Bellman. San Francisco: Berrett-Koehler, 1992. A guide to self-empowerment for anyone who is trying to bring about change in an organization without the advantage of formal power.

Getting to Yes. Roger Fisher and William Ury. New York: Penguin, 1981. Provides step-by-step strategies for mastering the art of successful personal and professional negotiations in which everyone comes out a winner.

Hartwick Classic Leadership Cases. Oneonta, N.Y.: Hartwick Humanities in Management Institute. The cases (and teaching notes) offer selections from a wide variety of literature, pairing excerpts from a classic work with a contemporary article on a similar issue, and include questions and summaries of the leadership issues involved.

An Invented Life. Warren Bennis. Reading, Mass.: Addison-Wesley, 1993. Discusses the essence of leadership by bringing together various works by Bennis—written over the course of three decades—in a very personal, candid manner.

Lead! Richard Lynch. San Francisco: Jossey-Bass, 1993. Shows how to transcend the sometimes overwhelming everyday tasks that public and nonprofit managers must face to begin to lead, bringing out the best not only in themselves but in the people with whom they work and in their entire organization.

Leadership. James MacGregor Burns. New York: HarperCollins, 1978. This Pulitzer Prize–winning work has become one of the cornerstones of leadership as a field of study. In it, Burns lives up to his reputation as political scientist and historian, offering some break-through concepts surrounding issues of leadership's power and purpose, the origins of leadership, transforming leadership, and transactional leadership.

Leadership and Management of Volunteer Programs. James C. Fisher and Kathleen M. Cole. San Francisco: Jossey-Bass, 1993. One of the rare books geared toward leaders of volunteer programs, it makes current management research, theory, and literature relevant to volunteer administration.

Leadership and the New Science. Margaret J. Wheatley. San Francisco: Berrett-Koehler, 1992. Presents a unique, eye-opening perspective on organizational management based on some of the revolutionary discoveries taking place in today's science, including quantum physics, chaos theory, and biology.

Leadership Is an Art. Max DePree. New York: Doubleday, 1989. This thoughtfully and elegantly written book is packed full of wisdom, revealing the human side of leadership.

Leadership Jazz. Max DePree. New York: Doubleday, 1992. Writing in the same style as *Leadership Is an Art,* DePree creates a unique link between leadership and jazz music, stressing the importance of the connection between one's voice and touch.

Leadership Secrets of Attila the Hun. Wess Roberts. New York: Warner Books, 1985. In a storytelling fashion, Roberts makes the unlikely characterization of Attila the Hun as an individual from whom leadership lessons can be extracted and used by today's managers.

Leadership Without Easy Answers. Ronald A. Heifetz. Cambridge, Mass.: Belknap Press, 1994. Offers leaders and potential leaders at all levels a practical approach to leadership, recognizing that this crisis of leadership we are now facing has been caused as much by unrealistic demands and expectations as from any leader's inability to meet them.

Learning to Lead. Jay A. Conger. San Francisco: Jossey-Bass, 1992. As a means of looking at the role training programs play in leadership development, Conger shares the experiences he had with five of the nation's most popular leadership training programs and the results one can expect from them.

Love and Profit. James A. Autry. New York: Morrow, 1991. Combines two of Autry's interests—poetry and management—into a meaningful book that looks at the human side of management, paying special attention to the wide variety of difficulties managers face every day.

Making a Difference. Sheila Murray Bethel. New York: Putnam, 1990. An inspiring work that shows—through the presentation of twelve leadership qualities—how we, as individuals, can make a difference in our personal lives, work lives, and communities.

Moral Leadership. Thomas J. Sergiovanni. San Francisco: Jossey-Bass, 1992. On the topic of improving the leadership in schools, this book discusses how a school can be transformed from an organization to a community by dedicating itself to a new leadership practice focusing on a common purpose, values, and belief system.

The New Leaders. Ann M. Morrison. San Francisco: Jossey-Bass, 1992. Using sixteen U.S.-based private and public organizations as examples, Morrison delves into those practices that encourage and those that discourage the advancement of women and people of color in the workplace, discusses the benefits of valuing diversity, and provides a step-by-step diversity action plan for organizations.

On Leadership. John W. Gardner. New York: Free Press, 1990. Based on five years of field study of organizations and interviews with hundreds of leaders, this book offers an examination of leadership issues critical to the dilemmas of today, exploring "the issues behind the issues," including motivation, values, social cohesion, and renewal.

Real Power. (Revised Edition.) Janet O. Hagberg. Salem, Wis.: Sheffield, 1994. Takes a new look at power in relation to leadership, describing six stages of personal power: powerlessness, power by association, power by symbols, power by reflection, power by purpose, and power by gestalt. (To obtain a copy of the "Personal Power

Profile," contact Personal Power Products, 1735 Evergreen Lane North, Plymouth MN 55441–4102, (612) 551–1708.)

The Seven Habits of Highly Effective People. Stephen R. Covey. New York: Simon & Schuster, 1989. An inspiring work that guides you through principles that, once learned and understood, can provide an integrated approach to both personal and professional problem solving.

Spirit at Work: Discovering the Spirituality in Leadership. Jay A. Conger and Associates. San Francisco: Jossey-Bass, 1994. Recognizing the increasing changes in the environment, society, and the workplace, this book examines the role spirituality can play in leadership, stressing the spiritual potential that organizations possess.

Straight Talk for Monday Morning. Allan Cox. New York: Wiley, 1990. With a format of short, punchy chapters and numerous sections throughout the book on how to take action, Cox offers ideas and values to help pull any organization together and begin truly functioning as a team.

Taking Charge. Perry M. Smith. Garden City Park, N.Y.: Avery, 1988. Provides a very down-to-earth, practical guide for coping with the myriad dilemmas that leaders of large, complex organizations face every day.

The Tao of Leadership. Lao-tzu. Adapted and translated by John Heider from the Chinese *Tao Te Ching.* New York: Bantam Books, 1985. Written in a style of elegance, poetry, and meaning, this work provides an adaptation—for all aspiring leaders of today—of the laws of effective leadership set down by an ancient Chinese sage.

They Don't Get It, Do They? Kathleen Kelley Reardon. New York: Little, Brown, 1995. Through numerous examples, Reardon confirms for women in the workplace the feeling that there is a communication gap between the sexes. She offers practical suggestions for how women should respond to different perceptions, objectives, statements, and body language in ways that will help advance their careers.

They Shoot Managers, Don't They? Terry L. Paulson. Berkeley, Calif.: Ten Speed Press, 1988. Presents practical management and leadership techniques for handling change and conflict, designed to help improve relationships, morale, and energy levels.

The Web of Inclusion. Sally Helgesen. New York: Doubleday, 1995. Offers a broad, revolutionary approach for bringing management out of the nineteenth century and into the present by looking at today's organizations as webs that are natural, organic, and constantly changing.

Zapp! The Lightning of Empowerment. William C. Byham with Jeff Cox. New York: Harmony Books, 1988. Through the telling of a fable, this book offers simple, straightforward methods that managers, supervisors, and organizations can employ to truly empower the people with whom they work, thereby increasing quality, customer satisfaction, and productivity.

| Audio and Video Programs

Source for videotapes and films: *Leadership Education: A Source Book, 1994–1995.* F. H. Freeman, K. B. Knott, and M. K. Schwartz (eds.). Greensboro, N.C.: Center for Creative Leadership, 1994, pp. 421–434.

Audiotapes

Taking Charge. Audiotape authored by Perry M. Smith. Produced by John Cominos. Niles, Ill.: Nightingale-Conant, 1992.

The Tao of Management. Audiotape authored by Bob Messing. Narrated by Ralph Blum. Commentary by Ken Blanchard. Produced by Audio Renaissance Tapes, 1990; distributed by St. Martin's Press, New York.

Videotapes and Films

Bolero. 1972. Runtime: twenty-eight minutes. Distributor: Pyramid Film & Video, P.O. Box 1048, Santa Monica CA 90406–1048, (800) 421–2304. A dramatic film relaying some of the finer points of leadership through a portrayal of what goes into a musical performance (a magnificent effort by the Los Angeles Philharmonic). Comments from soloists, concertmaster, and conductor Zubin Mehta are included.

Breaking the Glass Ceiling. 1993. Runtime: thirty-four minutes. Distributor: Video Publishing House, Inc., Four Woodfield Lake, 930 N. National Parkway, Suite 505, Schaumburg IL 60173–9921, (800)

824–8889. An inspiring video for women who want to learn from fellow risk takers how to gain self-awareness and how that glass ceiling can be broken. It includes a twenty-four-minute discussion starter, a ten-minute case study, and a training notes guide.

The Business of Listening. 1991. Runtime: twenty-five minutes. Distributor: Crisp Publications, Inc., 1200 Hamilton Court, Menlo Park CA 94025–9600, (800) 442–7477. Based on the book by Diane Bone, it covers the basics of effective listening, providing both suggestions and interviews with those knowledgeable on the subject.

C and the Box: A Paradigm Parable. 1993. Runtime: seven minutes. Distributor: Pfeiffer & Company, 8517 Production Avenue, San Diego CA 92121–2280, (800) 274–4434. Based on the book by Frank Prince, this brief session-starter is designed to assist people in breaking out of ruts and allowing their creativity and problem-solving skills to grow and develop.

The Credibility Factor: What Followers Expect from Leaders. 1990. Runtime: twenty-two minutes. Distributor: CRM Films, 2215 Faraday Avenue, Carlsbad CA 92008, (800) 421–0833. James Kouzes and Barry Posner, authors of *The Leadership Challenge,* offer advice on how to build credibility, fulfill the expectations of followers, and create a trusting and productive environment.

Ethics in America. 1988. Runtime: sixty minutes. Distributor: Annenberg/CPB Collection, P.O. Box 2345, South Burlington VT 05407–2345, (800) 532–7637. This is a series featuring close to a hundred panelists who grapple with various issues of ethics and values. Individual titles: *Do unto Others; To Defend a Killer; Public Trust, Private Interests; Does Doctor Know Best?; Anatomy of a Corporate Takeover; Under Orders, Under Fire, Parts 1 & 2; Truth on Trial; The Human Experiment;* and *Politics, Privacy, and the Press.*

Even Eagles Need a Push. 1992. Runtime: twenty-four minutes. Distributor: CRM Films, 2215 Faraday Avenue, Carlsbad CA 92008, (800) 421–0833. Based on his book, David McNally offers five qualities necessary for success and confidence: self-appreciation, vision, purpose, commitment, and contribution.

Joshua in a Box. 1969. Runtime: six minutes. Distributor: CRM Films, 2215 Faraday Avenue, Carlsbad CA 92008, (800) 421–0833. This short film is designed to be used as a discussion starter on the topics of human needs, control, and much more. With no narration, it portrays the story of a character trapped in a box, finally escaping the box, then becoming a box himself and trapping another character.

The Leader Within with Dr. Warren Bennis. 1989. Runtime: sixty-four minutes. Distributor: Video Publishing House, Inc., Four Woodfield Lake, 930 N. National Parkway, Suite 505, Schaumburg IL 60173–9921, (800) 824–8889. Three remarkable leaders of large organizations are interviewed by Bennis, offering their own personal views of leadership.

Leadership Skills for Women. 1991. Runtime: twenty-five minutes. Distributor: Crisp Publications, Inc., 1200 Hamilton Court, Menlo Park CA 94025–9600, (800) 442–7477. Based on the book by Marilyn Manning and Patricia Haddock, this video encourages women to become leaders in both their professional and personal lives, and offers examples of women leaders who have done so.

The Man Who Planted Trees. 1987. Runtime: thirty minutes. Distributor: Direct Cinema Limited, P.O. Box 10003, Santa Monica CA 90410–9003, (800) 525–0000. An award-winning animated version of Jean Giono's book, it tells the story of a widowed peasant who plants a hundred trees a day for thirty years, although he knows only one-tenth of them will survive. The result is a thriving ecosystem, teaching the value of persistence and the impact individuals can have on large goals.

Meetings, Bloody Meetings. 1993. Runtime: thirty minutes. Distributor: Video Arts, Inc., 8614 West Catalpa Avenue, Chicago IL 60656, (800) 553–0091. This is an updated version of a video that takes a humorous look at meetings that waste time, while also offering demonstrations of techniques for making them more efficient.

Rainbow War. 1986. Runtime: twenty minutes. Distributor: Pyramid Film & Video, P.O. Box 1048, Santa Monica CA 90406–1048, (800)

421–2304. This award-winning animated film tells the story of three kingdoms—the Blue, the Red, and the Yellow—who fight for ultimate supremacy. In the end, however, all three are winners and a lesson on valuing differences and collaboration is learned.

Take Me to Your Leaders. 1990. Runtime: forty-seven minutes. Distributor: Pyramid Film & Video, P.O. Box 1048, Santa Monica CA 90406–1048, (800) 421–2304. Hosted by James Garner, this program provides an optimistic view of the future through the observation of the creative leadership of several young people.

A Tale of "O": On Being Different. 1993. Runtime: training version eighteen minutes; presentation version twenty-seven minutes. Distributor: Goodmeasure, One Memorial Drive, 16th Floor, Cambridge MA 02142, (617) 621–3838. Rosabeth Moss Kanter and Barry Stein explore issues of diversity. Through the widely applicable use of X's and O's, they make the viewer aware of what it is like to be the few among many.

Valuing Relationship. 1993. Runtime: thirty minutes each. Distributor: Griggs Productions, 2046 Clement Street, San Francisco CA 94121, (415) 668–4200. This is a three-part series that uses science as a means of describing relationships as more than their unrelated parts—as ecological systems, each part intricately woven with the next. Titles: *Organizational Energy, Personal Patterns,* and *Interpersonal Synergy.*

You. 1980. Runtime: four minutes. Distributor: Cally Curtis, 24 Rope Ferry Road, Waterford CT 06386, (800) 522–2559. Narrated by William Schallert, this film takes a humorous look at the lessons we learned as children but somehow lost along the way to adulthood. Via scenes of a baby exploring a room, the viewer is encouraged to recapture that knowledge.

Notes

Unless otherwise noted, all quotations from leaders are taken from personal interviews, from personal written cases, or from public stories told by the leaders and analyzed by the author. The titles and affiliations of the leaders in this study may be different today than they were at the time the manuscript was submitted for publication.

Chapter One
1. Cronin, T. E. "Thinking and Learning About Leadership." *Presidential Studies Quarterly.* New York: Center for the Study of the Presidency, 1984, *XIV*(1), 29.
2. Bennis, W., and Nanus, B. *Leaders: The Strategies for Taking Charge.* New York: HarperCollins, 1985, p. 222.
3. Heifetz, R. As delivered at 1994 Leadership Conference, Harvard University.
4. Quoted in McNally, D. *Even Eagles Need a Push.* New York: Delacorte Press, 1990, p. 109.
5. "Address of Senator Robert F. Kennedy: Day of Affirmation" at University of Capetown. Press Release, June 6, 1966.
6. Briand, M. "People, Lead Thyself." *Kettering Review,* Summer 1993, p. 39.
7. Briand, M. "People, Lead Thyself," p. 39.
8. DePree, M. *Leadership Is an Art.* New York: Doubleday, 1989, pp. 23–24.
9. Quoted in Xaviermineo, H. "A World We've Only Dreamed Of." In P. Barrentine (ed.), *When the Canary Stops Singing: Women's Perspectives on Transforming Business.* San Francisco: Berrett-Koehler, 1993, p. 178.

Chapter Two
1. Turnbull, W., with Manly, H. *Lift Every Voice: Expecting the Most and Getting the Best from All of God's Children.* New York: Hyperion, 1995.
2. Work, D. P. "Voices of Angels." *Sun-Sentinel.* Feb. 20, 1994, pp. 1D, 4D.
3. "Profile: A Short History." *The Boys Choir of Harlem, Inc.* Press kit materials, received Aug. 31, 1995.

4. Work, "Voices of Angels," p. 4D.
5. "Biography: Walter J. Turnbull." *The Boys Choir of Harlem, Inc.* Press kit materials, received Aug. 31, 1995.
6. DePree, *Leadership Is an Art,* p. 3.
7. Smith, P. M. *Taking Charge: Making the Right Choices.* Garden City Park, N.Y.: Avery, 1988, p. 85.
8. Smith, *Taking Charge,* p. 85.
9. Bennis, W. *On Becoming a Leader.* Reading, Mass.: Addison-Wesley, 1989, p. 51.
10. Bennis, *On Becoming a Leader,* p. 40.
11. Gardner, J. W. "The Moral Aspect of Leadership." *Leadership Papers/5.* Washington, D.C.: Independent Sector, Jan. 1987, pp. 10–16.
12. Gardner, J. W. *Self-Renewal: The Individual and the Innovative Society.* New York: HarperCollins, 1963, p. 13.
13. Lao-tzu. *The Tao of Leadership: Leadership Strategies for a New Age.* Adapted and translated by J. Heider from the Chinese *Tao Te Ching.* New York: Bantam, 1985, p. 65.

Chapter Three

1. DePree, M. *Leadership Jazz.* New York: Doubleday, 1992, pp. 8–9.
2. Bryson, J. M., and Crosby, B. C. *Leadership for the Common Good: Tackling Public Problems in a Shared-Power World.* San Francisco: Jossey-Bass, 1992, p. 32.
3. Rost, J. C. *Leadership for the Twenty-First Century.* Westport, Conn.: Praeger, 1991, p. 109.

Chapter Four

1. Kelley, R. E. *The Power of Followership.* New York: Doubleday, 1992, p. 203.
2. Lee, C., and Zemke, R. "The Search for Spirit in the Workplace." *Training.* Minneapolis, Minn.: Lakewood Publications, June 1993, p. 22.
3. Lee and Zemke, "The Search for Spirit," p. 22.
4. Ritscher, J. A. "Spiritual Leadership." In J. Adams (ed.), *Transforming Leadership: From Vision to Results.* Alexandria, Va.: Miles River Press, 1986, p. 61.
5. Ritscher, "Spiritual Leadership," p. 61.
6. Lee and Zemke, "The Search for Spirit," p. 25.
7. Scott, K. T. "Leadership and Spirituality: A Quest for Reconciliation." In J. A. Conger and Associates, *Spirit at Work: Discovering the Spirituality in Leadership.* San Francisco: Jossey-Bass, 1994, p. 83.
8. Scott, "Leadership and Spirituality," p. 83.
9. Scott, "Leadership and Spirituality," pp. 83–84.

10. Miller, W. C. "How Do We Put Our Spiritual Values to Work?" In J. Renesch (ed.), *New Traditions in Business: Spirit and Leadership in the 21st Century.* San Francisco: Berrett-Koehler, 1992, p. 77.
11. Covey, S. R. *Principle-Centered Leadership.* New York: Summit Books, 1990, p. 94.
12. Covey, *Principle-Centered Leadership,* p. 94.
13. Covey, *Principle-Centered Leadership,* p. 95.
14. Miller, "How Do We Put Our Spiritual Values to Work?" p. 71.
15. Griffin, J. H. *Black Like Me.* Boston: Houghton Mifflin, 1961.
16. Rabbin, R. "Leadership and Spiritual Inquiry." *World Business Academy Perspectives,* 1992, *6*(2), 39.

Chapter Five

1. Bennis and Nanus, *Leaders,* p.27.
2. Nanus, B. *Visionary Leadership.* San Francisco: Jossey-Bass, 1992, p. 156.
3. Bennis and Nanus, *Leaders,* p. 28.
4. Briand, "People, Lead Thyself," p. 40.
5. Briand, "People, Lead Thyself," p. 40.
6. Nanus, *Visionary Leadership,* p. 156.

Chapter Six

1. Johnston, W. B., and Packer, A. H. *Workforce 2000: Work and Workers for the 21st Century.* Indianapolis, Ind.: Hudson Institute, 1987, pp. 85, 89.
2. Johnston and Packer, *Workforce 2000,* p. 95.
3. Covey, S. R. "Value the Differences." *Executive Excellence,* 1994, *11*(11), 3.
4. "Fast Facts." *Changing Scene,* 1995, *4*(2), 5.
5. Cortés, C. E. "Backing into the Future: Columbus, Cleopatra, Custer, and the Diversity Revolution." *Higher Education Exchange.* Dayton, Ohio: Kettering Foundation, 1994, p. 7.
6. Peck, M. S. *The Different Drum.* New York: Simon & Schuster, 1987, p. 73.
7. Peck, *The Different Drum,* p. 74.
8. Gozdz, K. "Building Community as a Leadership Discipline." In M. Ray and A. Rinzler (eds.), *The New Paradigm in Business: Emerging Strategies for Leadership and Organizational Change.* New York: Putnam, 1993, p. 108.
9. Blake, R. R., Mouton, J. S., and Allen, R. L. *Spectacular Teamwork: How to Develop the Leadership Skills For Team Success.* New York: Wiley, 1987, p. 2.
10. Blake, Mouton, and Allen, *Spectacular Teamwork,* p. 2.
11. Much of the material that follows was inspired by Bruce W. Tuckman, "Development Sequence in Small Groups," *Psychological Bulletin 63,* 1965, and by Peter R. Scholtes and others, *The Team Handbook,* 1988.

12. Arendt, H. "Power and the Space of Appearance." *Kettering Review,* Summer 1993, p. 18.

Chapter Seven

1. Batten, J. D. *Tough-Minded Leadership.* New York: AMACOM, 1989, p. 60.
2. Acevedo, R. As delivered as a panel member to the Kellogg National Fellowship Program Group XV Fellows in Lake Bluff, Ill., June 6, 1995.
3. Bennis and Nanus, *Leaders,* p. 43.
4. Bennis and Nanus, *Leaders,* p. 43.
5. Mayo, E. Quoted in Reynolds, J. *Out Front Leadership.* Austin, Tex.: Mott & Carlisle, 1994, p. 80.
6. Fittipaldi, B. "New Listening: Key to Organizational Transformation." In Barrentine (ed.), *When the Canary Stops Singing,* p. 228.
7. Fittipaldi, "New Listening," p. 228.
8. Fittipaldi, "New Listening," p. 228.
9. Fritz, R. *You're in Charge: A Guide for Business and Personal Success.* Glenview, Ill.: Scott, Foresman, 1986, pp. 74, 76.
10. Smith, P. *Taking Charge: How to Make Things Happen in Your Organization.* Audiotapes. Niles, Ill.: Nightingale-Conant, 1992.

Chapter Eight

1. Klopp, H., with Tarcy, B. *The Adventure of Leadership.* Stamford, Conn.: Longmeadow Press, 1991, p. 119.
2. Klopp with Tarcy, *The Adventure of Leadership,* pp. 115–119.
3. *Merriam-Webster's Collegiate Dictionary.* (10th ed.) Springfield, Mass.: Merriam-Webster, 1993, p. 398.
4. Dodge, C. "Ethics Watch: Jerry's Kids." *Ethics: Easier Said Than Done,* 1995, *29,* 3.
5. Dodge, "Ethics Watch," 3.
6. Clark, K. E., and Clark, M. B. *Choosing to Lead.* Charlotte, N.C.: Leadership Press, 1994, p. 51.

Chapter Nine

1. *Daily Thoughts for School Administrators.* Cambridge, Mass.: Principals' Information and Research Center, May 14, 1979.
2. Serling, R. J. *Legend and Legacy: The Story of Boeing and Its People.* New York: St. Martin's Press, 1992, pp. 128–131.
3. *Executive Speaker,* 1995, *16*(6), 8.
4. Bethel, S. M. *Making a Difference: Twelve Qualities That Make You a Leader.* New York: Putnam, 1990, p. 136.

5. Olesen, E. *Twelve Steps to Mastering the Winds of Change.* New York: Macmillan, 1993, p. 195.
6. Lear, N. Quoted in Bennis, *On Becoming a Leader,* pp. 148–149.
7. McCall, M. W., Jr., Lombardo, M. M., and Morrison, A. M. *The Lessons of Experience: How Successful Executives Develop on the Job.* Lexington, Mass.: Lexington Books, 1988, p. 19.

Chapter Ten

1. Gardner, J. W. *On Leadership.* New York: Free Press, 1990, pp. 2–3.
2. Covey, S. R. *The Seven Habits of Highly Effective People.* New York: Simon & Schuster, 1989, p. 109.
3. Cox, A. *Straight Talk for Monday Morning.* New York: Wiley, 1990, p. 56.
4. Hagberg, J. O. *Real Power: Stages of Personal Power in Organizations.* (rev. ed.) Salem, Wis.: Sheffield, 1994, p. ix.
5. Hagberg, *Real Power,* p. ix.
6. Paraphrased from Gemmill, G., and Oakley, J. "Leadership: An Alienating Social Myth?" *Human Relations,* 1992, *45*(2), 123.
7. Paraphrased from Gemmill and Oakley, "Leadership," 123.
8. Quoted in Bennis, W., and Mische, M. *The 21st Century Organization: Reinventing Through Reengineering.* San Diego, Calif.: Pfeiffer, 1995, p. 98.
9. Quoted in Batten, J. D. *Tough-Minded Leadership.* New York: AMACOM, 1989, p. 23.
10. Lao-tzu, *The Tao of Leadership,* p. 155.
11. Hagberg, *Real Power,* p. 160.
12. Pitkin, H. F., and Shumer, S. M. "On Participation." *Kettering Review,* Summer 1994, p. 21.

Chapter Eleven

1. Tucker, R. B. *Managing the Future: The Essential Survival Tools for Business in Today's Market.* New York: Berkley, 1991, pp. 99–100.
2. Tucker, *Managing the Future,* p. 100.
3. Tucker, *Managing the Future,* p. 100.
4. *Hope Health Letter,* 1995, *XV*(5), 6.
5. *Executive Speaker,* June 1994, p. 4.
6. Cited in Olesen, *Twelve Steps,* pp. 31–32.
7. Peters, T. *Thriving on Chaos: Handbook for a Management Revolution.* New York: HarperCollins, 1987, p. 324.
8. Gamerman, A. "Ex-Rocker Converts His Musical Talents into Heavenly Niche." *Wall Street Journal,* Aug. 15, 1995, pp. A1, A6.
9. Whitehead, B. "Illinois Town Finds Its Future in the Past." *Evansville Courier.* Feb. 7, 1994, p. A4.
10. Whitehead, "Illinois Town Finds Its Future," p. A4.
11. Whitehead, "Illinois Town Finds Its Future," p. A4.

12. Young, R., and Power, G. "Self-Sustaining Communities." *In Context,* Fall 1992, (33), 10.

Chapter Twelve

1. Braham, J. "Lighten Up." *Industry Week,* Mar. 7, 1988, p. 51.
2. Feigelson, S. "Mixing Mirth and Management." *Supervision,* Nov. 1989, p. 6.
3. Peters, T., and Austin, N. *A Passion for Excellence: The Leadership Difference.* New York: Warner Books, 1985, p. 296.
4. Feigelson, "Mixing Mirth and Management," p. 7.
5. Leatz, C. A., with Stolar, M. W. *Career Success/Personal Stress: How to Stay Healthy in a High-Stress Environment.* New York: McGraw-Hill, 1993, p. 185.
6. Filipczak, B. "Are We Having Fun Yet?" *Training,* April 1995, p. 50.
7. Filipczak, "Are We Having Fun Yet?" p. 50.
8. Hugo, V. Quoted in *Daily Thoughts for School Administrators.* Cambridge, Mass.: Principals' Information and Research Center, Mar. 21, 1979.

Chapter Thirteen

1. Smedes, L. B. *A Pretty Good Person.* New York: HarperCollins, 1990, p. 174.

Resources

1. Senge, P. M. "The Leader's New Work: Building Learning Organizations." *Sloan Management Review,* Reprint Series, Fall 1990, *32*(1), 7.

Index